A Man's Torn Heart

The Loss of an Angel to Breast Cancer

Alan E. Lobdell
Cover Art by Bryan P. Lobdell

CLASSIC DAY
PUBLISHING

Seattle, Washington
Portland, Oregon
Denver, Colorado
Vancouver, B.C.
Scottsdale, Arizona
Minneapolis, Minnesota

ISBN: 1-59849-024-9
Library of Congress Control Number: 2006935195

Printed in the United States of America

Cover Art: Bryan P. Lobdell

Editor: Katherine Grace Bond
Design: Soundview Design Studio

Classic Day Publishing
2925 Fairview Avenue East
Seattle, Washington 98102
877-728-8837
ewolfpub@aol.com

Dedicated to the love of my life, Maxine Alvanos Lobdell (formerly Maxine Pangburn), who shared more joy and love with me in the five years two months and thirteen days that she was in my life than I had ever experienced. I love and miss her more than anyone will ever know; however, I know she is in Heaven with our Lord Jesus, as she always knew she would be, and this comforts me.

Acknowledgements

◆ ◆ ◆

I would like to thank all those who have made my life bearable during these difficult years:

To our kids, Scott, Chris, Bryan and Aolani, who have always been there to talk. To Rick and Kathy Parton — Kathy was Maxine's partner and cheerleader in fighting breast cancer; they both fought the disease the best they knew how. To Terry and Susan Newby — Terry has been by my side since I met him on my 50th birthday, September 24, 2001; Susan is a powerful prayer warrior whom Maxine counted on hundreds of times. To Doug and Janet Boese — Janet was always there for support and was another prayer warrior when Maxine needed it. To New Community Church in Maple Valley, Washington for their incredible support, which continues even as I write; I sometimes believe that my sanity would have been lost if not for the loving, generous people of this church, led by Pastor Ken Mitchell and his wife, Valerie. New Community Church truly lives up to the meaning of Christian charity. To Point Man

Ministries — just a bunch of hurting veterans who have become so close to me that I can openly say I love those guys. To my family, who gave 100% support in whatever way we needed, even though many times they did not believe in what we were doing. To my copy editor, Aolani Glover Erickson, who corrected all of my mistakes. To my consultant, Barbara Nichols and her fifteen plus pages of ideas. However, my most heartfelt thank-you goes to my editor, Katherine Grace Bond, who made my ramblings sound like something intelligent. And to another hundred or so people who touched our lives during our battle with cancer.

Table of Contents

◆ ◆ ◆

Chapter 1   The Discovery 1

Chapter 2   Finding the Love of Your Life 7

Chapter 3   The Beginning: Love at First Sight 13

Chapter 4   The First Doctor's Appointment 31

Chapter 5   The Lumpectomy 39

Chapter 6   Standard Medicine Cannot Help....................49

Chapter 7   A Dream Vacation 57

Chapter 8   Going Natural 67

Chapter 9   Cost Problems 79

Chapter 10   Intensified Natural Treatment........................85

Chapter 11   Relatives, Church and Friends........................97

Chapter 12   Our Last Fun Trip 109

Chapter 13   The Healing Rooms 117

Chapter 14   Optimum Health Institute (OHI)
             April/May 2002 129

Chapter 15   Radiation and Chemotherapy 147

Chapter 16   Her Faith in Jesus 163

Chapter 17   Germany: A Lost Hope 169

Chapter 18   OHI 2003 179

Chapter 19   Coming Home the Last Time.......................187

Chapter 20   The Memorial..199

Chapter 21   Three Years after Loss 207

Conclusion: The Challenge 221

Bibliography..223

Editor's Note

◆ ◆ ◆

It has been a privilege to edit this book. I have come to love Maxine Alvanos Lobdell, not only through her husband's writings, but through being entrusted with video footage, photographs and her journal. I grieved her loss, though I never met her in person.

There is a death that all of us must face and either fight or give in. Alan Lobdell has never given in: not in Maxine's battle with cancer, not after her death. He is fighting not only for Maxine's life and memory, but against the soul-death of despair.

I like this book because it is honest. Alan does not candy-coat anything. He gives the full story. Through his years of struggle, Alan has learned to cut away the trivial matters we focus our energies on and find what is truly important. If you are struggling, you will find a brother-in-arms in Alan. His compassion, loyalty and insight can give you strength to carry on.

Katherine Grace Bond

Foreword

◆ ◆ ◆

I have written this book not for the breast cancer patient, but for the husband of the patient, for he, too, is a victim and is very often forgotten by those concerned with his wife's affliction. Of all the difficulties I have encountered over the last five years, writing this book was one of the most challenging. With each line I remembered details of what we went through and the pain was almost unbearable. I could only write for a couple hours at a time or I'd get too emotional and upset to continue.

I spent over a year thinking about whether I should even try to write a book about my experiences fighting this disease. Many friends and relatives told me that I should put everything down in writing so that other men could get some help from what I have already gone through. Writing this meant I had to remember all the problems we faced, the heartache of knowing the cancer was growing and the hopelessness that it put in my heart. Watching this incredibly beautiful woman, who I loved so much, become weaker and weaker until she could no longer stand and had to be in a wheelchair was almost more than I could take. She was 49 years old, yet seven months before she died she was able to pass for 35.

Chapter One begins with a short essay (The Discovery) I wrote one afternoon in June of 2002. We had been fighting the cancer a little over two years at that time. Maxine was out shopping with her daughter (Aolani) and I was at home alone. I was always worried about her when I was not in sight of her, and was pacing back and forth in the house.

Rather than pace all day long, I decided to sit down at the computer and start writing my feelings. The difficulty of this is that guys are not supposed to show their feelings. Yeah, I know. I've heard all that stuff about letting your "feminine side" come out. Well, that's just a bunch of bull to a guy like myself. I'm sure it is to a lot of you guys who grew up the old way and have a very protective side when it comes to your wife and family. The men out there who are experiencing what I went through will understand.

I have been a civil engineer for almost thirty years and have always looked for the logical way to approach any and all problems. I found, much to my dismay, that you cannot approach cancer in a logical manner. The affliction has no logical pattern and that's what makes fighting it so difficult. As a man it was my job to provide for and protect my family. This is what I was brought up to believe and still do. However, with cancer there is no one and nothing to fight; there are only ghosts and you have no way of hitting them. How can you fight against a virus — or whatever cancer really is?

This is the mental place where I was during the entire time

we were fighting for Maxine's life. In many ways I am still there. I was in terrible emotional pain seeing her get weaker each year and there was nothing I could do about it. My job was to hold her and tell her I loved her and be there with her at every doctor appointment and procedure she had to endure.

It was beyond any doubt the most difficult time in my life, but I would give anything, even go through it all again, just to have her back with me for one hour — just to make sure she knew how much I loved and miss her.

God willing, I will see her again someday. That's God's promise and I'm holding Him to it.

I hope the rest of this book detailing some of the experiences we had and what I went through will help you if you are unfortunate enough to be placed in the same circumstances. Some of the mistakes I made will haunt me forever, so I have tried to point out those mistakes within these pages. I hope I will be able to help you to get through the pain and heartache by letting you know that you are not alone. If, after you read this, you believe talking with someone may help, please feel free to contact me at my e-mail address, Alvanos@juno.com, and I will respond.

I know that writing this book is a big task. My goal is that I don't want any man to have to go it alone ever again. May God bless you! *I know your pain!*

Alan E. Lobdell
July 31, 2006
Covington, Washington

CHAPTER 1

The Discovery

◆ ◆ ◆

There's nothing like knowing your life could be cut very
short to get you to start appreciating every single day.
You start to see more beauty in the everyday things.
It's like crossing over into a different realm entirely.

— Maxine

There you are guys, lying in bed with your wife — the woman you love more than anything else in the world. You have been married anywhere from ten minutes to 60 years. In my case it was almost two years.

The sun was starting to come in the bedroom window and it appeared that a beautiful day was blooming. I looked over at my wife, Maxine, who was still somewhat asleep. She looked so peaceful and beautiful and I thought to myself just how lucky I was to have someone like her to love and hold. I could hear birds outside and I knew that there wasn't any reason to rush. In my mind I was planning us a day trip to the ocean or mountains or zoo. Maxine woke and snuggled up to me. Did I ever love the feel of her warm, soft body. She loved to crawl all over me and hold me as tight as she could. She wrapped her legs around me and it was almost like there was only one body in the bed. Did that ever feel good! She had no idea how excited she could get me with just a special look. I put my arm around her to hold and caress her. I could feel the softness of each part of her and I was in a state of total relaxation as she responded to my touch. I slowly and very gently caressed her warm, soft breast and could feel her starting to get excited. Everything in the world was perfect.

I was about to make love with the woman of my dreams and it did not matter how many times we had made love before, it was always like the first time. My skin was getting goose bumps in anticipation. And then something happened to change everything: I felt a strange lump in one of her breasts.

I slowly caressed the breast trying to determine if the lump was really there. Maybe I was hoping I could make it go away. My mind raced to the most terrible thought I could have: cancer.

What should I do now? What should I say? Should I tell her? Keep quiet and hope I was imagining it? Should I scream?

I lay there in a sweat, unable to remove my hand from the foul spot. Maxine was talking ever so sweetly to me but I heard nothing of what she was saying. I was engulfed in fear. My mind was already racing ahead and showing me standing alone in life without my lovely lady. The thought was almost more than I could stand.

How would I tell the kids, Maxine's mother, sister and brother? What would I tell them? I felt like I had died a thousand deaths.

"Alan, what's wrong?" Maxine was puzzled.

I tried to speak calmly. "Give me your hand, baby."

I directed her hand to the location of the thing I had found. When I placed her fingers on it I felt like I'd died another thousand deaths. Now another entirely different set of fears ran through me and they all came from the fear I could see in her eyes. There, under her fingers, was the lump. I could not wish it away or ignore it. The pain in me was the worst that I had ever felt: nauseating, empty, longing, loss, hunger. Maxine was simply too young and beautiful to have something like cancer growing within her body.

STRENGTH

If you are unfortunate enough to have found something like I found in my wife, you understand the feelings I had. I am here to tell you it can consume you and completely overpower you if you allow it. At that point you will be at the mercy of fear.

This is something you had better address from the very beginning: *You will have to allow others to be strong for you.* You must do this for you, and especially for your wife. She needs you more than ever before and that means you need someone for support also. For you to be strong for her, you will need to allow someone else to be strong for you.

If you have never read the Bible, I would strongly recommend it to you. You may not believe in the Bible and maybe not even in God, but you will find a world of good, soothing and helpful words that will give you hope and help you to survive the coming years.

Who knows? It may even put you on the road to belief. You simply cannot read God's history and not be deeply affected by it. The history and word of Jesus will give you the strength needed following your discovery. I know this for a fact; I was only beginning to know the Lord when all of this started. I have leaned on His Word throughout and it has helped me to keep my sanity. I have never been loud or boisterous about it, and I've usually prayed in private, but I have felt deep relief and comfort from this. You, too, may only want to pray in private — so do it! It's okay. You need it.

No matter what else happens, no matter what anyone tells you or what you read, never, never, ever give up hope. It's all you have, and you must never let your wife see you or hear you act or sound like there is no hope, or that you have given up.

If you feel that way at times (and I guarantee you will), it's all right. Just do it somewhere off by yourself or with a friend who can be trusted.

I've had to make excuses to take one to two-hundred-mile driving trips by myself just to allow myself to work out my distress. I'm sure I am quite a sight to those who don't know when they see me talking to myself and/or crying in the car, driving down the highway. Yes, guys, I said crying. I was nearly fifty years old when my wife got cancer. I'm six feet tall and weigh 200 pounds. I am an ex-Marine, skilled in martial arts and I worked out every day to stay hard. Yet when I was alone I'd cry like a baby at the thought of my wife having this disease because *I was completely helpless against it.* You, too, will feel this helplessness and my advice is to allow yourself to cry. Again, it's OKAY!

DESPITE OUR BEST INTENTIONS

There will come a time when you will do the exact opposite of what you want to do. Yes, this sounds strange, but it's true. A number of times after we discovered the cancer I found myself saying or doing things to hurt Maxine. Afterwards I'd look at myself and ask, *Why did I say or do that?*

Believe me, it will take every bit of strength you have to watch out for these times and avoid them. They will happen. You must work this out and put an end to it. Until this happens to you, I'm sure you will not understand what I am saying, but just keep this little story I'm telling in the back of your mind and you will remember it when it happens. When it does, it's up to you and you alone to fix it. I know it happens because of the stress and pressure and fear you have been living with, but keep in mind that for her it's much worse. And you, my friend, have only hurt her more when it happens. I have done this too many times myself.

When you do find yourself hurting her, give her some time alone, then go to her and hold her. Tell her that you are sorry and that you will make a concentrated effort to never let it happen again. Then stick to what you say. Oh yes, never stop telling her how beautiful she is and how much you love her. If you just said it today, say it again. She needs that more than anything else in the world. Remember it's only the beginning and I'm sorry to say it can get much worse. Just hang in there and you will be all right.

May God bless you in your cancer fight. There are those of us out there who have gone before you. We are just as lost but we are willing to talk; it helps us too. Look for us before you can take no more.

CHAPTER 2

Finding the Love of Your Life

◆ ◆ ◆

Prayer is a powerful reality.
— Maxine

The Bible says that there are angels walking amongst us. I am now convinced that I was married to one of these angels for almost five years. She came into my life unexpectedly and did what she was meant to do: change the course of my sons' lives, and mine, and then she left. I thank God every day for having given her to me, even if it was for too short a time.

CALLING INTO THE NIGHT

In August 1996, I was driving along Highway 12 from Richland, Washington heading for Chehalis. I had been in Richland for a meeting, a trip of 230 miles each way. I was working far from home and for three years had not been able to be home during the week. This was not altogether bad since my 22-year marriage was a mess; I knew a divorce was coming soon. But I longed every night to be with my sons, whom I loved very much.

It was 3:00 AM and I was on the mountain pass 100 miles from Chehalis when I felt very alone. For some reason I decided to look up at the sky. I leaned over the steering wheel. The night was clear and the stars were out. I was not even tired.

I had not gone to church since I was a young boy and I simply did not believe in anything, much less a God, so it was strange when I found myself praying.

"Okay God," I said, "if you are real, let's see you get me out of this bad marriage and bring my life together, along with bringing a woman into my life I can love and trust."

Little did I know how that prayer would be answered. Be careful what you pray for — you just might get it.

Within a month of that night I was falsely accused of some improper dealings at work and was sent home on administrative leave, pending an investigation. Only later did I discover that the man at fault was conducting the investigation. In November of 1996 I was fired. (It took ten months and the involvement of an investigating prosecutor from the state capital to clear me of all charges.)

These events left me looking for another job, which I found in January of 1997. It was only a one-year contract, but at least I was working.

I didn't know that news of the problem in my past job was traveling rapidly around the Northwest. I learned once my one-year contract was over that I had been black-balled from almost every city, town and county in the Northwest. Everyone had heard or read about the accusations, but no one ever read the little article in the paper ten months later explaining that I had not been at fault.

In March of 1997, I filed for divorce and moved into a two-bedroom apartment. During this time I dated very little and tried to keep working and paying off bills.

ON A WHIM

The fun started one night in October of 1997 when I heard about a dance for singles being held down on the pier in Seattle. I drove there, but almost went home due to no parking places. I was actually driving away when there, off to the side, I saw a parking spot. I watched at least ten other cars looking for parking drive by that same spot as if it was not there. It was as if that spot was meant for me.

I went into the dance and found it to be a lot of fun. There were lots of people and I love to dance. During a break I discovered that because we had paid to get into the dance, we were allowed two weeks of free singles ads. I had been married for 23 years and had never heard of such a thing. *Okay*, I said, *I'll try it as a joke.* I signed up that night and forgot about it.

Several days later I received instructions in the mail to call in and place a phone voice message about myself for my singles ad. I thought that it was a waste of time, but I did make the message as they had instructed. Again I thought, *What a joke.* Well, what a shock I was in for. Over the course of the two weeks my ad was in the paper I had about 45 messages. What really shocked me were the calls from doctors, dentists, lawyers, and other professional women. I called each back to at least be polite and even set up dates for coffee with six of them. They were all very pretty, shapely women, but I just did not feel right with any of them.

Discouraged with that, I decided I did not want to meet any more, except for the very last message I received. The woman — "Roberta", she said her name was — sounded very nice and so I called back only to get her 83-year-old mother. Roberta had already told her mother that she was not going to respond if I did call, but after talking with me, her mother promised that she would *make* her daughter call back.

And she did.

"Roberta" and I talked for an hour. She was feisty and liked it that my kids were so important to me. She, herself, had a daughter starting college. "How do your kids feel about other women being around?" she asked.

"My kids will take to somebody in a heartbeat if I like them and they treat me good," I told her.

She thought about this.

Finally, we agreed to meet in a local restaurant. "What color is your hair?" I asked her.

"What color would you like?" she shot back sassily.

FINDING THE LOVE OF YOUR LIFE ◆ 11

What am I getting into? I thought.

That Sunday I arrived at the restaurant fifteen minutes early. Twenty-five minutes later there was still no Roberta. Feeling "stood up," I left.

She called later and she didn't sound sorry at all. She had arrived seconds after I left. "I saw your name scratched out on the register," she said. "I was really disgusted that you couldn't even wait fifteen minutes for me."

Be nice, I thought. *Say good-bye and never worry about meeting this woman.*

"Can we try again?" she said.

No! I thought. "Well," I said. "I'm in the middle of moving and I'm doing a lot of stuff."

"What would be a good time?" she persisted.

"Couple of weeks," I lied. "I'll call in a couple of weeks."

Two weeks later, my sons were helping with my move and my oldest son, Scott, came outside. "That woman is on the phone," he said, nodding toward the house.

Oh great, I thought, *just what I need.*

"You weren't going to call me, were you?" she said.

I started unpacking the dishes. "No."

"Why not?"

I stacked plates. "Because you stood me up."

"That's your version," she said. "Besides, we talked for an hour before. We seemed to get along."

I sorted forks and spoons. "Yeah, but..." I said flatly.

"Can't we just meet and have coffee?" she teased.

"All right," I said vaguely. "Whatever." I set the empty carton on the floor. Couldn't she just give up?

"When?" she said.

"Whenever."

"Six," she said. "Tonight. Seattle's Best Coffee."

"Yeah, okay." I hung up the phone. *God,* I thought, *I don't want to talk to that woman.*

At 6:00 I was at the counter buying coffee. *Get in, get out,* I thought. *Meet her, be polite, let her down easy.*

"Hi Alan!"

I turned. She was standing just a few feet from me: auburn hair, blue eyes. She had on a black pleated skirt with a white ruffled blouse and a red blazer. She was absolutely a knockout.

I fumbled my coffee, spilled it, grabbed for napkins, dropped my money. "Roberta's" smile lit up the room. The sales girl started laughing. I threw a five on the counter and stammered, "Take whatever you want."

Of course everyone in the shop was now looking and laughing at me. It didn't matter; I was in love. Or lust. Or something. I couldn't take my eyes off her and I wanted to know her more than I had wanted anything in my life.

CHAPTER 3

The Beginning: Love at First Sight

◆ ◆ ◆

I know God has a perfect plan for my life.
I submit to Him.
— Maxine

When we first sat down I was so taken by her that I had a hard time even thinking of something to talk about. "Roberta" sipped her white chocolate mocha. She chatted amiably, perfectly at ease. After a few minutes I woke up and, to my horror, realized that she was far too young for me. I had put in my ad that I was looking for someone close to my age so that we would at least have similar life experiences to talk about. "Roberta" couldn't be more than 33. And I was 46.

Get in, get out; let her down easy. Ha! Now I didn't want to leave. But it was too much of an age difference. It couldn't work.

"Listen," I told her finally. "I find you very beautiful and sweet. I'm attracted to you. But you're too young for me."

She smiled. "When were you born?" she asked me.

I told her.

She set her cup down and looked straight at me. "I'm only a year and a half younger than you; what's the problem?"

There was no way I was going to believe she was 44 years old. "All right," I said. "Let's see your driver's license."

She smiled again and pulled it out. "I've had my ID checked many times in my life, but this is the first time I've had to show it to get a date."

Once I looked at it and saw her birth date I was so embarrassed.

She just laughed. "It's a wonderful compliment," she said.

We sat and talked for an hour that first date and set up two more dates later that week. Not many people believe in love at first sight, but that was how it was for Maxine and me. At least that's how I felt and I was pretty darn sure she felt the same way. However, I did not know this for certain until over a year after she died when my son found a book in which she had written everything about our first meeting. What a joy it was to find and learn that she also fell for me the same instant. In fact, she had even written in her book that she had to force herself not to ask me to marry her on our second date. The book was called *The Rules* and she was playing me by the book for the first three dates. Then there was a last notation that said, "This is not by the rules, but I don't care. I love talking to him." That was the last thing she bothered to write about in *The Rules* book.

PERFECT FIT

Our third date was in early February of 1998. We had been out until about 11:30 PM. The roads had become very slick with black ice and I was barely able to keep my van on the road. We went to my townhouse since it was close and decided to wait and see if the roads would get any better. After an hour I told her that I had better try to get her home to her place.

"Alan, no," she said. "It's bad enough getting me home on this ice, but then you'd have to drive back here. I'll just sleep on the couch."

That old couch felt like a rock and I was not about to let her sleep on it. At the time I had my oldest son living with me in the second bedroom.

"Look," I said. "I'm happy to have you stay here, but you are not going to sleep on the couch and be miserable."

Her eyes widened a little. She knew where I was going.

"I've got some sweats you can wear," I reassured her. "And I'll wear sweats too."

"Alan…" she had a stubborn set to her jaw.

"I won't bother you," I told her. "I give you my word."

She hesitated, looked at the couch, then at me. Her face softened and I grabbed her hand and took her upstairs.

I was sound asleep when somebody grabbed me. It was

Maxine, sitting straight up. "What am I doing in your bed?!" she yelled.

I looked up at her, groggily. "Is anyone bothering you?"

"No," she said.

"Good. Then stop waking me up and go to sleep."

Maxine lay back down, snuggled up to my back and slept. By morning she had both arms wrapped around me as tight as she could.

Years later she told me that she must have had more trust for me than anyone she had ever known since her father to have done that. She didn't know at the time that I was so afraid of screwing up our relationship that night that I would never have done anything to upset, hurt or make her mistrust me.

Maxine and I knew we were going to be married by that third date. We just seemed to fit with each other's lives in a way that I could only describe as perfect. By the way, she was a red-head when I met her, but within a month she informed me that she had been blonde all her life and that the red hair was just a new thing to have a change in her life from her own past bad marriage. She asked me if I would mind her going back to blonde. I had never even dated a blonde up to that point in my life but I was willing to try just about anything with her. Once she became a blonde, her real beauty came out. I was amazed that such a gorgeous woman would want to be married to me. Maxine had long, thick beautiful blonde hair that glimmered in the sun.

When we drove anywhere I would laugh at guys of all ages almost breaking their necks trying to get a second look. And when she would put on her short white shorts with her always-tanned legs, she almost always caused a problem. I was so proud of her and I told her every day how beautiful she was. She laughed at me when I did because she, in all honesty, did not realize how good she looked. Then again, maybe she did.

She put *The Rules* book away and we went looking for wedding rings. Maxine worked at a major department store in Seattle and had been checking in Fine Jewelry regularly for just the right setting. She asked me to come look at a few she liked.

While we were there I noticed something in the far back that Maxine had not noticed. It was a men's gold wedding band with a cross on it. When I tried it on, it fit like it was made for me.

"I love that!" said Maxine. "I wish there was one like it for me."

"Look back in the case; there's a matching one."

The clerk took it out for her.

Maxine examined it in the light. "Wouldn't it be strange if it fit me the way that one does you?" She put it on and her eyes got as big as dollars. An exact fit.

"We'll take them!" We said it almost simultaneously.

The clerk rang the rings up. "I'm curious," Maxine asked him. "I've been in here almost every day. Why didn't I see these before?"

He smiled. "They weren't here before today. We just put them in the case this morning."

I don't think we talked at all until we got to the truck and sat there looking at each other. Maxine was shaking her head. "Alan, this is too much. What do you think is going on here?"

"I think we're supposed to get married."

THE WEDDING

Maxine and I did not announce our marriage plans until about a month and a half prior to the wedding. My divorce would be final on March 18th of that year. My three sons were delighted at the news. Anything or anyone that made their dad happy was okay by them. They also adored Maxine and she loved my sons. Understand that these guys were 16, 18 and 20 years old, and somewhat protective of their dad. However, it didn't take long before they preferred her to Dad and sided with her on everything.

Telling Maxine's daughter was another story. She had watched her mom in a poor marriage situation for about seven years and was shocked that her mother would even consider marrying a man she had known less than six months. She was very upset, and in no uncertain terms let us know about it. She did, however, calm down rather quickly and was a great help with the wedding. All four of our kids were involved with our planning and the wedding went smoothly because of them. We also found out that her daughter and my middle son had graduated from high school together. As it turned out, Maxine's daughter (Aolani) and my three sons (Scott, Chris, Bryan) became like brothers and sister very quickly. My sons thought it was "cool" to have a sister and I believe she thought it was nice to have brothers.

Maxine and I were married on May 24th, 1998, only four and a half months after we met, at Rosario Resort on Orcas Island. Our wedding was a simple gathering of our best friends and some relatives. We had arranged for the ten members of the wedding party to be flown from Renton to Rosario in float planes. That would allow everyone in the wedding to get there and home in one day. Anyone driving would have to take the ferry and some were going to stay overnight. My oldest son, Scott, had driven my van over the day before and towed my trailer with Chris's 1100 Honda motorcycle in it for Maxine and I to use after the wedding. Scott would then fly home in my place on the plane. It was a beautiful setting and ceremony and not even the rain cast a shadow on our special day. Aolani served as Maid of Honor and Scott as Best Man. The wedding was not without those endearing faux pas that make a special event memorable.

The ceremony went fine until we got to the vows. Somewhere in the middle of them Maxine drew a total blank. Aolani looked at Scott and suppressed a chuckle. The pastor tried to cue Maxine, but she was stuck. Aolani and Scott concentrated on their feet, trying to preserve the solemnity of the occasion.

Finally, Maxine jumped to the next line she remembered, "I will be his best counsel..." and added, "...if I can get my mouth to work."

So much for decorum; the place just broke up. Scott was bent over laughing and I could no longer control myself. To Maxine's credit she turned to me, giggling, and whispered, "And I told you four times not to forget your lines!"

This should have told us that things could get even better.

We were about halfway through the reception luncheon when my son Scott came over and whispered, "Dad, I think that old man down there died."

Down at the end of the table an older man was lying with his face in a bowl of soup. Scott had good reason to think that this could ruin the wedding, but it wasn't what he thought. The gentleman was Maxine's stepfather and he was 82 years old. He had Narcolepsy: he could fall asleep at any time, even while talking to you. I reached over and pulled him out of the soup; Maxine cleaned his face, and we propped him up comfortably. He never even stirred.

Our next reception surprise happened a short time later; however, our kids and friends chose not to tell Maxine and me about it. It seems one of our guests had been enjoying his dinner salad when he noticed it moving. He reached in and picked out a slug three inches long, placed it on a napkin and continued eating. Apparently Aolani had seen the slug and immediately took it back to the kitchen, where she had a few choice words with our host. Everyone at that table quietly received a new salad.

You would think there had been enough small problems for one wedding, but we had one more to go. The escort staff dis-

THE BEGINNING: LOVE AT FIRST SIGHT ◆ 21

appeared. Instead of the bride and groom being able to take off and be alone, we ended up directing people to their cars, loading planes and making sure everything at the reception was picked up and taken care of. It took us about an hour to get everything done so that we could finally leave and go to our room. As I look back on it I can only say that we had a perfect wedding in a beautiful place and everyone had a great time.

To Love and Trust

I believed that we had almost everything a couple could ever want in a marriage and Maxine's diary states that she felt the same way. Life was fun and we were gone somewhere almost every weekend. We traveled around the state and enjoyed everything we could. Maxine and I believed in staying healthy and watching everything we ate. We both stayed on a special diet plan, ate organic foods and went to the gym together to work out at least every other day. We wanted to stay in great shape for each other. We enjoyed the same movies and we both loved the outdoors. We knew that we would be together for a long time.

During that first year together we were making good money and were able to pay off all of our debts, so we decided to purchase forty forested acres of land up in Okanogan County. Our property was about halfway between the small towns of Tonasket and Republic. It lay about thirty miles south of the Canadian border and was at an elevation of about 4500 feet. It was perfect in our eyes; it had a bench on the highest side about 200 yards across before it gently sloped down into a valley. When standing at the top of the bench we could see our entire forty acres along with the valley for about 20 miles. We had deer, moose, bear, cougar, and a multitude of other animals. The chipmunks and squirrels were always right there watching us and looking for food.

The summer of 1999 we drove 300 miles one way each Friday to work on the cabin we were building there and drove home each Sunday. It was a long and tiring ride, but we loved being together in our little Toyota truck. Maxine, a lifelong Christian and Bible College graduate, spent most of the time in the truck at her pulpit preaching to the newly converted heathen she had married.

"Listen, Alan. This is First Thessalonians 4:6. 'Let your speech be always with grace, seasoned with salt, that ye may know how ye ought to answer every man.' This is why we need to be forgiving and gracious when wronged. See, here in Luke 6 Jesus says, 'Be ye therefore merciful, as your Father also is merciful. Judge not, and ye shall not be judged; condemn not, and ye shall not be condemned. Forgive and ye shall be forgiven. Give, and it shall be given unto you; good measure, pressed down, and shaken together, and running over, shall men give into your bosom. For with the same measure that ye mete withal it shall be measured to you again.'"

She was always after me about forgiveness. It was a very big thing for her. She wanted me to not feel so mean toward some people. She kept telling me that I would feel better if I forgave.

One day I would see how important forgiveness was. At the time I was too bone-headed to understand.

After about five to six hours of her preaching, I would ask, "Can we talk about anything other than the Bible for the last hour of the drive?"

Maxine's sermons happened every time, with the exception of the few times that she had worked so hard that she fell asleep as soon as we started home. Although I loved listening to her, there were times when the silence was nice.

Building our cabin became a big part of our life for about six months. We were up at the property every weekend once we got started. That first night we spent up there under the stars was an interesting night that I will always remember. We had driven through snow and mud most of the way. It was spring, but at the 4500 foot level the snow was still heavy. We pitched our tent under some trees that had sheltered the ground from the snow. Maxine prepared a nice steak dinner over our Coleman cook stove. She could make the best meals on that little cook stove.

Later that night, when it was time to go to sleep, I discovered that my girl was not the outdoorswoman I had been led to believe. After most of my life of hunting for deer and elk I was very used to sleeping in a tent. She was not used to this. Every time anything made the slightest noise she would scream and grab me.

"What's that?"

"Probably a raccoon; go back to sleep."

Then later…

"Aah!"

"It's a bird, Max; go to sleep."

And after I'd drifted off…

"Alan!"

"Maxine, I have my rifle right next to me; we're not in any danger. Don't wake me up again unless something is coming through the wall of the tent."

"Coming *through* the tent?"

Don't ever tell your wife something like that if she is not used to camping. I thought I was having a hard time sleeping before I said it; well, there was no chance of sleep after I said it.

The next morning Maxine very willingly took her first shooting lessons.

I had purchased her a rifle several weeks earlier that she would be able to shoot easily since it did not recoil like a normal rifle. It was a Chinese-made SKS and I had also picked up a thousand rounds of ammo along with eight to ten thirty- and forty-round clips. She was a little afraid at first but got the hang of it very fast and after some practice she was able to hit a six-inch bull's-eye at fifty yards anytime she wanted. She found to her liking that she was able to shoot a lot of rounds very fast. I explained to her that I had bought hollow-point rounds and that there was nothing up there these would not stop rather fast. The second night I was able to get some sleep because she had the rifle next to her with a 30 round clip in it (on safe, with no round in the chamber, of course). She kept it there every night we had to sleep in the tent.

Once she was comfortable sleeping in the tent she began to see it as romantic. Again sleep was difficult, but I didn't care anymore.

When we first started planning, Maxine was not able to understand how we were going to build this cabin, nor was she able to visualize what it would look like. I explained that it would be 24 feet long and 20 feet wide with a 12-foot loft, however that explanation again was too vague for her. I decided to draw up some plans to show her exactly what I had in mind. I drew a floor plan showing the size and where the doors and downstairs windows would be located. Well, Maxine was more of an artist than an engineer, so to her the floor plan didn't get the job done. Frustrated, I took one afternoon to complete an isometric drawing of the cabin I envisioned for us. That worked; she now had a good idea of what we were going to build. It gave her an idea of what she was going to want for windows. She seemed to be very concerned about the windows. I was not sure why until later when I found out exactly what she wanted.

I picked the highest point of our property to build the cabin and set the back wall facing the west to look out over our land and the valley below. I set the cabin up on stilts, two feet high in the front by the door and approximately five feet high in the back. This was to accommodate the gentle downward slope and keep the cabin level. My intent was also so that it would be above the snow and keep critters out. Chipmunks, squirrels, mice and other little critters were everywhere and always around the cabin when we were working.

The first floor was going to be the main part of the cabin. I was planning on a metal spiral staircase that I could buy complete and install. The stairs would go up to the 12-foot by 20-foot loft that would be a bedroom and storage. I wanted the main bedroom upstairs and she wanted it downstairs. Guess who won that one?

It wasn't until the second weekend of work that Maxine actually started believing that we were going to build a cabin. Saturday morning I was up early and working on building wall frames. She was cooking breakfast by Coleman stove and looked up just as I tilted the first full frame. She dropped what she was doing and came running. She threw her arms around me screaming, "We're going to build a cabin!"

I got all four wall frames up that weekend and we were on our way. She was really into it from that point on. The weather was hot and by Sunday noon we were both dirty and sweaty. I had found a nice stand of small trees where I made an outdoor shower with tarps. I then placed a pallet on the floor of the shower and covered it with a piece of plywood so that we would have a place to stand and the water would drain. We had two five-gallon Coleman camp shower bags that we would leave out in the sun all day and when we were ready for our first mountain shower that second Sunday, the water in the bags was hot. It was great. There's nothing like taking an outdoor shower in the mountains with your wife. Especially when there is no one else around for miles and she knows it. The week before we had been tired, hot, sweaty and smelly driving home, but the second week we were relaxed and feeling great.

Back home Maxine was going from yard sale to yard sale looking for bargains for our cabin. I was at work one morning when she called very excited and told me that I had to go with her that evening and pick up some windows she had purchased at a contractor's yard sale. I had no idea what to expect and was very surprised to see that she had bought seven brand new Milguard windows for only $25 apiece. Two of the windows were 6-foot by 5-foot or bigger. Seems the contractor purchased the wrong size for a house he was building and, of course, Maxine talked him out of them for a fraction of the price he'd wanted. She could find bargains or work deals better than anyone I have ever known. They would look great on our cabin, and believe me she already knew exactly were she wanted each one of them. There would be no choice on my part.

It may sound funny that much of what we used on and within our cabin came from Maxine's ability to find things at yard sales, but it did save us a lot of money. She would go to a couple of them each day while I was at work. Or if we didn't go to the cabin to work on some weekend I knew that a few hours of my time would be taking her to her yard sales.

One Saturday she had talked me into looking at yard and estate sales all day long, and had so far purchased nothing. We stopped in at a little house where she knew there was an estate sale going on. The old couple that lived there had died and apparently had no relatives. A company was selling everything in the house. I was bored out of my mind by the time we got there, but she had agreed that this was the last one for today. Okay, I could handle this last one. She went in; I looked at the junk for about five minutes and went back to the car to read.

Finally, Maxine came out, got in the car and said, "We can go now." She had purchased a small box of twenty-year-old stationery for fifteen cents.

I flipped out. "*That's* what you bought? I drove you all over creation for *that?*"

"Just be quiet and drive, Alan."

I started driving all right, but I would not shut up. "We've spent *five hours* doing this. You spent an entire hour in that house alone and it was nothing but garbage."

Maxine just sat there and smiled at me. I should have known something was up.

Finally, she looked at me and opened the box of stationery. She started flipping through the pages of old paper. The paper was nothing to look at; what made it worth looking were the twenty-dollar bills stashed between the pages.

Maxine never said a word. All I could do was tell her that I would never complain about her yard sales again.

We worked on our cabin every weekend we could that summer and managed to get it to about 90 percent complete. We made it up there one last time in 1999 to put a tarp over the roof until we could get the tin covering on it in the spring. Looking out our picture window we could see all the way down the valley. In the morning we would have breakfast in clear sky while the valley would be a sheet of fog. This is when we started planning on the future additions to the cabin. One day we would be able to retire and live there. It was a beautiful dream and we talked about it almost every day. The next spring we would finish the tin on the roof and put up the log siding and build the deck. She wanted French doors going out to the deck facing the downhill and valley view. I was not sure how I was going to do it, but we could at least dream about it. After October of 1999 we could no longer get up to the cabin due to almost three feet of snow. That was okay with us; we were going to wait for spring and be ready to go to work again.

I guess all really good things must come to an end, because in December, 1999, all of our hopes and dreams came crashing down and we were left in a fearful state of mind, not knowing what the future would hold for us.

CHAPTER 4

The First Doctor's Appointment

◆ ◆ ◆

*God is leading me even though I'm walking through the
valley of the shadow of death. He is there to comfort me
and to dispel the torment of fear by His perfect love.*
— *Maxine*

The morning we found the lump was to be a fun one of taking a drive and playing; instead it became a very serious one of phone calls and setting up appointments. Maxine was very methodical about calling all around and finding what she felt was the right breast cancer clinic to go to. This was one woman that never did anything without studying the situation very carefully. We were both scared of what might be growing within her, but still hopeful that it wouldn't be anything serious. We had agreed that only after talking to the doctor would we inform Aolani. It was still possible that it was nothing.

The doctor and clinic Maxine chose were in Seattle and somewhat well-known. Once the appointment was made, all we could do was wait. The five or six days seemed like forever. I was a nervous wreck, but I could not let her see that for fear that it would only make things worse for her. I covered up my fear as best I could and tried to act like I was in complete control. The fact was I wanted to scream and hit something.

I was so terrified that I didn't want to accept the lump was even there. I wanted to take Maxine and run away from it. I believed that I needed to hide my feelings from her, but I now believe that this was a mistake. I should have let her know how much turmoil I had going on inside me. It would have shown her more about how much she meant to me.

GUT REACTION

The day of that first appointment finally came, but once we saw the doctor I did not get a good feeling about him. In fact, I did not want her seeing him at all. I can't explain this feeling, but it was there. Have you ever felt that you did not want to trust someone the very moment you met them?

In the past Maxine had always listened to me when I got these feelings, but this time she didn't.

The doctor talked to us at length about the lump and insisted on having a mammogram done so that he could see more clearly what was there. This would be the one and only mammogram Maxine would ever allow to be taken. Reports from European countries that we read stated that compressing the breast for a mammogram would release cancer cells from the tumor into her blood stream. Our reading led us to believe that ultrasounds and MRI's were much safer.

After the mammogram the doctor told us that because of the shape of the lump, it did not look like cancer to him. He said maybe it was a benign tumor that may not ever cause any problem. This seemed strange to me, especially since we had told him that the lump had not been there even two months earlier. (Or at least we had never found it, and Maxine was somewhat careful to check for breast lumps.) I had never heard of a benign tumor growing that fast, but I was sure willing to hope he was correct.

He wanted her to have a needle biopsy taken right then to determine the makeup of the tumor. In a needle biopsy they deaden the area around the breast and then push a long needle into the tumor and extract a small portion of it. I was against this simply because I did not trust the doctor. Mind you, at that time I had no real reason to feel that way other than a "gut instinct."

Maxine, however, thought he was wonderful. "You're being silly, Alan. I trust him completely. You need to calm down."

Well, at that point I shut up. Later I would wish to God I had stuck to my feelings and made her find someone else.

The needle biopsy did not take all that long to do, however, the report we got in an hour or so was non-conclusive. The doctor told us that they were unable to extract enough of the tumor and would now have to do what I believe he called a "core biopsy." This meant cutting into her breast and taking a larger sample from the tumor. It could not be done that day since she would have to be put under a general anesthetic.

Maxine was upset that we could not get an appointment for several weeks. She was very scared and wanted to know as soon as possible what was growing within her. I did not mind the timing of the biopsy; it was who was doing it that bothered me. As it was, three days later the doctor's office called. They had a cancellation for the next day and wanted to know if Maxine would like to take it. She jumped at the chance to get in weeks earlier than we had expected. It was now mid-December of 1999.

SURGERY

The need for the core biopsy was more than we had expected and we decided that we could no longer keep this to ourselves. Maxine informed her mother, Aolani, and other relatives of what we had found. I in turn called each of my sons and relatives to let them know. Breast cancer was new to both of our families and everyone was very concerned.

The day of the core biopsy came and Maxine and I were very nervous. She had never had any kind of surgery in her life and was afraid of going under general anesthesia. I was a pro at surgeries since I'd had about ten, so I was able to calm her down a little. However, if anyone at the clinic had taken my pulse they would have thought I was about to explode. While we were waiting for her to go in, a woman came out and asked me to accompany her to a little room.

"Since you don't have insurance, Mr. Lobdell, we require 50% of the total cost up front."

Well, I knew that was coming and I had the cash in my pocket. "So," I asked, just for the fun of it, "What would you have done if I did not have the money?"

Her answer was short and sharp. "I would have Maxine's surgery cancelled and you would have to leave."

Wow! With this attitude along with my mistrust of the doctor, I was *ready* to take Maxine and leave.

I paid and Maxine went in as scheduled. Maxine's daughter, mother, her sister, an old friend, her brother and I waited out in the little room they had for the families. I was miserable. All I could do was pace back and forth like a caged animal, knowing that if it was cancer I was helpless. I had never felt so useless in my life. I walked, I prayed to myself, I drank coffee. I wanted so much to get my wife and leave that place and not have any of this happen. It was like the start of a nightmare and I was unable to wake up. I was hurting so bad and yet I could not let anyone see that. Call it my pride or whatever, that was the way things were. I felt that if I let anyone, especially her family, see me so emotional they would think of me as weak.

Maxine was not in surgery very long since it was a relatively simple procedure. She was in the recovery room within an hour and actually waking up within an hour and a half. I was allowed in to see her, along with Aolani. She was awake and smiling as best she could but still somewhat under the effects of the drugs given for the surgery. She sat up and tried to talk to us but was not able, so she just grabbed each of our hands and held on tight. She wanted the two of us as close as possible. We had about an hour to wait for the results of the biopsy, so Aolani and I left to allow others to come in and see her.

After awhile a nurse came out and told Aolani and me to come back because the doctor wanted to talk to us. I got a bad feeling about that. Maxine was sitting up feeling somewhat better and now wide-awake. She had me on one side and Aolani on the other when the doctor told her that the lump was indeed cancer. He also told us that during the operation he had not attempted to remove it since he had not planned to do a lumpectomy at that time. What he said meant that she needed to have the lumpectomy as soon as possible to avoid any more spread of the cancer cells than had already been done by cutting into the tumor.

At that time I was unsure of exactly what he was telling us, but I later understood that he had created a situation where the cancer was now in her bloodstream in larger volumes than when the lump encapsulated it. As we learned later, he should have removed the entire lump at that time, and after talking to many other women from several other clinics we discovered that Maxine was the only one that had been treated in that manner. All of the other women told us that their doctors took the lump out on the first surgery.

At the news of the cancer Maxine broke down crying, and all I could do was hold her. I was dying inside and I'm sure Aolani was also. The three of us just held onto each other for some time while Maxine cried. The fear I could see in those beautiful blue eyes cut through me so bad and I was unable to do anything about it. After a while she wanted to see her mother and sister, so we left. Once out of sight Aolani had tears in her eyes and I walked up and put my arm around her. This was the first time she had ever let me hold her and she hugged me very tight, saying in my ear, "I don't want my mom to be sick."

Even though it felt like someone had stabbed me, I did all I could to conceal my fear and pain — you know, like a man is supposed to, right?

Wrong!

THINGS TO REMEMBER:

◆ Don't hide how you are feeling completely from your wife. I now think that I should have let her know just how scared I was. I believe she would have loved to know how I felt.

◆ Let others know, too. You don't need to break down like a blubbering fool, but I believe now that we, as men, should let others know how much we are hurting. You will be able to deal with the life and death issues much better if you allow yourself to show others how much she means to you. Believe me, it's not weakness; it's love. It also allows others to know how to react to and treat you. If you show nothing, people may not know how to sympathize with you. Although I did not see it then, I believe now that they wanted to help, but were as frustrated and fearful as I was.

◆ If she has children, don't forget how much pain they may be going through and don't hide your pain from them. Be there for each other and even cry with them if you or they need it. Let it out. Let them know how much you love their mother. If I were able to do it over, Aolani and my sons would have been allowed to see how hurt I was. I believe now that it would have helped us all.

CHAPTER 5

The Lumpectomy

❖ ❖ ❖

Long ago I determined to forgive.
That frees me. It frees me to love.
— Maxine

Maxine and I decided to live each new day as if it was our last together. We hoped that the lifetime we had looked forward to would not be cut short, but we had no guarantees. We didn't know what was going to happen, but we wanted to do as much as we possibly could. We began to look at each day as a lifetime for us. Each day could bring renewed hopes and maybe the miracle we would need.

CHRISTMAS

Somehow we got through Christmas that year. The joy was taken out of most of us, but not Maxine. She never let us dwell on our circumstances. Even though we knew that she had to go back for a lumpectomy in January, there was no stopping her at

Christmas. This was her favorite time of year and she was determined to make the best of it. Our house was decorated from top to bottom and inside to out. She was not about to let cancer ruin her holiday spirit. She even made me drive all over the mountains that year until she found just the right tree to cut down and drag back.

And do I mean drag. We tramped all over in two feet of snow while Maxine looked at this tree, then that one. None was quite "it." Finally, she spotted the sorriest-looking tree I'd ever seen. "That one," she said.

I hauled out the saw. "You really like it?"

"Yeah." She lay down in the snow.

"You like it, I'll cut it."

She cocked her head at the tree. "It's got potential."

"It's pretty skimpy."

I cut the tree down and Maxine got a closer view. "I suppose we can't leave it here and pick another one."

I must have given her a look, because she shook her head. "Probably not," she answered herself. She stood up and brushed the snow off her legs. "Well," she concluded cheerfully, "that's the one, then."

Maxine loved that tree into something beautiful once we got it home. We had a great Christmas; the house was full of our kids and that's how she liked it.

AN EDUCATION

Maxine was always looking ahead and planning, but the one thing she had not planned on was breast cancer. She indulged herself in studying everything she could find on the subject. Before her lumpectomy she educated herself and me on every word and meaning in her pathology report. You know — the ones that are written in a language that no one can read or understand? Well, we read it very carefully and looked up words and phrases on the computer or in medical books until we understood what everything meant and what could and could not be done by the medical personnel.

Before the lumpectomy the doctor (still the one I did not trust) sent us to the hospital, where they inserted four titanium pins into Maxine's breast. These were to help in the locating and extracting of the tumor.

Another procedure was called the "sentinel node." They injected a radioactive dye into her. Whichever lymph nodes (usually two or three) the dye went to first were extracted and tested for cancer. This was a way to tell if the cancer had spread. We studied up on this so that we would understand exactly what would happen and what the results would mean.

THE SECOND SURGERY

The day finally came in January of 2000 for her to have the lumpectomy. This time, nearly all the same people were there except Maxine's brother since he was unable to get off work.

Again I had to pay 50% cash to have the surgery done and at that time I did not have as much cash on hand. I had to borrow most of it from my son, Chris. You can imagine how that made me feel.

Once paid, the woman at the window was all smiles. There was no sign at all of compassion or caring. It stirred up my feelings of not wanting Maxine in there; however, she had chosen the doctor, so all I could do was support her decision.

Aolani and I stayed with her up until they wheeled her into the operating room. The next hour was endless for me. Again I paced, I drank coffee, tried to read. I was scared to a point I had never been before in my life. I wanted to scream and smash things, but I couldn't do that. How would it look to the relatives sitting there quietly waiting? Were they as wrapped around the axle as I was? I didn't know.

Looking back I see that I should have asked them how they were doing and talked with them about the whole situation. It would have made things better for all of us. They were Maxine's family and I was the outsider she was married to. I was too self-involved to understand this at that time.

When she came out of surgery, again Aolani and I were allowed to go into the recovery room. She was still almost completely under but she knew who we were and grabbed us both and held on tight. Within a short time her wonderful smile came back and she really looked good. She was worried that she did not have any makeup on. Maxine was never seen without makeup for any reason. Thankfully, she got over that little problem and was in good spirits when the doctor came in.

The news was good; he said that they had gotten the entire tumor and obtained clean margins. That meant that no cancer was found around a certain distance from the tumor surgery area. The two sentinel lymph nodes that were taken out also showed no sign of cancer. Maxine was declared cancer-free.

This was almost too good to be true. Maxine and her family were extremely happy. I, on the other hand, was not all that thrilled. What about the prior surgery where they had cut the tumor and let all those cancer cells loose in her bloodstream? Yes, maybe they got all the cancer around the tumor but what about the other loose cells?

I was told I could take her home in a couple hours, once she completely woke up, and the nurse had time to teach me how to dress and care for the wound. We drove home and I got her settled at the house so that she could relax and recover. They gave her some pain pills, but she refused to take them. Maxine did not like taking drugs for any reason.

"Maxine, you've never had surgery," I insisted. "You don't know what you're in for."

"I'll be fine," she said.

That lasted only until the pain medication she had from the surgery wore off. Once the real pain started, she agreed to take the pain pills as directed.

I was so happy to have her home and see her smile again.

She had not smiled much at all since we first found the tumor. Maxine was a woman with a radiant smile that lit up a room when she entered. She was a naturally happy, cheerful person who loved everyone she met. She had more friends and could spread more love than anyone I have ever known. If she met someone and started talking to them they could tell within a couple minutes that she truly was interested in them and loved them.

QUESTIONING

About a week or so after the surgery we went back for a check-up and to talk with the doctor about what to do next. By this time Maxine was in full study of cancer and its treatments. She had recently finished reading a book called *Questioning Chemotherapy* by Ralph W. Moss, PhD (Former Assistant Director of Public Affairs at Memorial Sloan-Kettering Cancer Center and Founding Editor of The Cancer Chronicles newsletter).

Her doctor had told us on the first appointment with him that she would probably not need chemotherapy since they would be able to remove the tumor and get clean margins. However, he did say that radiation of the entire breast area to get any stray cancer cells was recommended. When he came in to talk to us at this first check up, his story had changed. He now recommended Maxine take a full course of chemotherapy along with radiation treatment.

What a shock this was to us. If I remember him correctly,

he told us that she should have the radiation first and then the chemo. We were confused by his change of mind. Why such a difference from what he had said before? He gave us a vague answer about random cancer cells.

I now know it was because of his earlier cutting into the tumor that he wanted her to take both treatments. This very doctor who had done the first biopsy knew by that biopsy report that chemo would not help. Maxine was also non-estrogen receptive, which meant other standard cancer treatments such as Tamoxifen would be ineffective as well. Now the doctor was trying to get her to take chemo. He even recommended a chemotherapist that he liked.

By this time we had learned a lot about cancer and its treatments. "Why," I asked, "are you recommending chemo when Maxine's pathology report shows a histolopathologic grade of 9 and a Her-2-Neu factor of negative? From what we've read there's not a chemo made that will affect the cancer she has." (For explanations see, "Understanding Your Pathology Report" on www.thebreastcaresite.com.)

The doctor didn't reply.

Maxine tried, "From everything we've studied, chemo works by killing all new cells that are developing — not just the cancer cells. Wouldn't the chemo destroy my immune system cells? It could make my body less able to fight the cancer."

He had no answer for us as he was too surprised that we knew this much about what the pathology report said and meant.

By this time I was furious and was trying to control myself. I wanted to drag him across that table and do a little bit of my own surgery on him. After the errors he had committed he had the nerve to tell us to poison her with something that could, in fact, kill her and have no helpful effect at all on the cancer.

We left the building, never to return. Maxine finally understood the feeling I'd had all along. She told me that she wished she had listened to me and gone elsewhere.

A few months later I was talking to some friends who had gone through the same thing with this doctor. However, they'd had the core biopsy and the lumpectomy along with the titanium pins and the sentinel nodes all done in the same surgery. When I looked into this, I discovered that doing it all at once was standard procedure. So, why were there two surgeries for Maxine?

I was finally able to figure out what I believe to be the answer: The others we talked to all had insurance. For them, everything was done in one surgery and their insurance companies paid about one-third to one-half. Some patients may have had a 10% co-pay, but after that, the bill was gone.

But we had no insurance. For each of Maxine's surgeries, I was required to pay 50% cash up front. Forcing us to pay cash up front gave them more payment than most insurance companies would pay, irrespective of the fact that I still owed the remaining 50%. By doing two surgeries they were able to get the 50% twice up front and again I still owed the remaining 50%.

In just one of the surgeries, the amount I was to pay was more than an insurance company would allow for both surgeries together. It was cost effective for them to schedule two cash surgeries no matter how much pain it caused Maxine.

My original bad feeling about this place and the doctor turned out to be true. Stick to your guns, men. If you have a bad feeling for any reason about a doctor, clinic or hospital, don't use them. I still feel guilty about not putting my foot down and insisting she go elsewhere. I know she would have had I been adamant about it. She always respected my feelings on things she knew I was serious about.

To make things even worse, we had bills from more than twenty providers from just those two surgeries. There were bills from the hospital, clinic, several doctors, labs, radiologists; the list seemed to go on and on. Maxine set up a payment program with each and was working on paying them off.

Nine months after the surgery the clinic sent us a notice stating that they had made a mistake and were now billing us for another $2500. I can assure you that I don't pay bills that come nine months after the fact. Furthermore, I proved that they did not make a mistake in their billing and that they were trying to over-bill us. This battle raged on for over a year because I stopped paying them altogether. My last letter to them was, "Back off or I will start a legal action for malpractice and uninformed consent." I never heard from them again.

Things to Remember:

◆ Study everything you can about her illness and treatments. This can combat your feelings of helplessness. You'll be doing what you can for her and keeping informed. It also gives her a sense of relief knowing that she does not have to fight alone. (At the end of this book there is a list of publications you may want to start with.) Do this before the doctors get started with treatment of any kind.

◆ Always have one person with you taking good notes whenever you meet with your doctors. There is no way for you to be able to remember everything that you are told. Even when two or three people are with you, what they hear can differ between them. You will find the notes very useful. If there are instructions, you will want them in writing for reference.

◆ I would advise anyone with a major medical problem to make every doctor, clinic, hospital or x-ray lab give you a copy of every paper, report or picture that is about you. I don't care what it is; you can demand copies. Then, study them all. Get help understanding them so you know exactly what they say and mean.

◆ Hang onto all of these papers and organize them by date, time and doctor. If you pay close attention to everything being said and done, you will want to refer to these as time goes by.

CHAPTER 6

Standard Medicine Cannot Help

◆ ◆ ◆

*The keys to overcoming and finding a path through
this jungle of natural healing options: an open mind;
a willing heart; careful, diligent personal research;
listening to professionals — both conventional and
alternative; much prayer for guidance; consistent
following of what you know brings positive results;
listening and learning from those who are winning their
own battle; keeping in mind we all have different types
of cancer and different responses/makeup; listening to
your innermost conscience/convictions.*

— Maxine

We were never going to go back to that doctor or clinic
again. Now we were on our own. For the time being
Maxine had been declared "free of cancer." Just to be safe, she
was going to go every three months and have blood tests done
at a local hospital. We had been assured that these tests were

able to detect cancer if it was to reappear. However, when we read up on them, the information we found said that they were not always correct. Still, it was all that was available for us. They were not that expensive and they gave Maxine something to hang on to, so we budgeted for them.

HEALTHY CHOICES

Not being willing to take any chances, Maxine proceeded to get every book, report or paper she could find on cancer and its treatment — both through standard medical and also natural methods. I wanted to support her as much as possible, so I would sit for hours reading along with her.

She and I had always been health conscious. We decided to go on an all-organic diet, along with juicing pure vegetable juice. The juicing idea came from a book by Lorraine Day, MD, *Cancer Doesn't Scare Me Anymore,* along with a number of VHS tapes Dr. Day had made about her battle with breast cancer. She explained that drinking pure, organic vegetable juice was a big part of her cancer battle.

After reading Doctor Day's book, Maxine wanted to get a good juicer as soon as possible. She found a website that compared all the juicers in the country and decided on one called The Green Life. It was an expensive juicer (about $650), but well worth it. I still have it today and it works as well as ever after juicing tons of vegetables over the years. I would recommend it to anyone who wants to juice and wants clean-up to be fast and easy.

During this time we learned a considerable amount about cancer and how it grows and spreads. As explained earlier, we had already discovered that Maxine's cancer had a makeup that was almost impossible for standard medicine to treat. Chemotherapy was not an option due to the location of her tumor and because the information on the pathology report indicated that it could not kill the cancer. Radiation was an option; however, Maxine had read a lot about radiation: it can kill cancer, but also can cause cancer by mutating the cells around the area so radiated. She was not ready to go that route yet.

She was out of options for any help by the standard medical system. Poison (chemotherapy), burn (radiation), or cut (surgery) were the only options available in the standard medical world. She had endured the surgery; the chemo, as we understood, would not work, and she did not want the radiation. Natural was all we had left.

SEEKING ADVICE

We still wanted to seek as much medical advice as we could, so we kept looking for and talking to different doctors, and people who had fought cancer. Some friends told us about Doctor Glenn Warner in Bellevue, Washington. He had been an oncologist for about forty years and was now consulting with people on cancer and other problems. We set up an appointment and were able to meet him that week.

Dr. Warner was around 82 years old and as sharp as anyone I had ever met. He really knew his medicine and told us that chemo and radiation were not the answer, even if the AMA thought so. He told us that oncologists and referring doctors got a cash bonus from the drug companies for each patient they signed up for chemotherapy. He said that doctors would tell you that they don't get the money but in his forty years of being an oncologist, he had never seen a case where they didn't. Wow! That sure told us something about the doctors we had been seeing. Even with the pathology report in hand, doctors tried to get Maxine to sign up for chemo. We had wondered why they would suggest that; maybe we had found out the answer.

Because of this information we decided to see what would happen if we tested a few doctors over the next couple of years. We would make appointments with oncologists and talk with them about Maxine's cancer. We would hand them a copy of the pathology report and ask what they would recommend we do. All but one said that they would recommend she start on a chemo treatment as soon as possible. We would then ask what kind of chemo that they would suggest. The overwhelming choice of chemo included one called Fluorouracil or 5FU for short. It was to be used by itself or mixed with others such as Cyclophosphamide, Vincristine, Methotrexate or Doxorubicin. (*Questioning Chemotherapy*, page 179)

I'm not going to try to explain what these are since that's not what this book is about, however you can look them up in a medical dictionary. The interesting part came when Maxine would sit back and smile very nicely and say, "So you want to use Five Feet Under on me? Now, why do you want to kill me?"

To say the least, the doctors were shaken up by the knowledge we had. You see, behind closed doors, doctors referred to 5FU as Five Feet Under. We could only guess why they call it that, but it does seem somewhat obvious. Could it be that these so-called wonderful medical doctors just wanted their bonus checks? We had no way of proving it but it sure looked that way to us. These doctors did not like us knowing this much about cancer or the pathology report or what it said. We were promptly asked to leave several offices after the conversation. At one office the doctor got up and left the room, never to return.

Only one of the doctors we talked to looked at the pathology report and then looked us in the eye and said, "I don't believe I can offer you much hope, because at this time there is no chemo that will help you." We never even found her until late into the third year of our battle. She informed us that there were many labs working on new versions of chemo that may, in the future, help with the kind of problems Maxine had, but that there was nothing for sure at this time. This doctor, from Swedish Medical Center in Seattle, Washington was the only one that we believe told us the truth from our first meeting, and because of that she is one of the very few we came to know and trust completely. She was to become Maxine's primary doctor during the last year of her cancer battle. We thank God for her honesty, even if she couldn't help.

One oncologist we visited locally was so convinced that he could get Maxine to sign up for chemo that he called her at our home three times trying to scare her into signing up for the treatment while I was at work. This doctor even had the gall to set up financing for us and called Maxine to inform her that we only had to pay $1100 per month for God only knows how long. I had to call his office and threaten to bring legal action if he ever called my house again.

Since we refused to sign up for his chemo treatments he had his billing office add over a hundred dollars to the bill for our consultation. Prior to setting up an appointment I had called and gotten a quote: it was from $135 to $185 just to speak to him. When I got the bill, it was over $300. I informed them that I would only pay up to $185. When I would not pay any more, he actually started legal action. That was fun since I had all my information very complete and when I presented it to the court, and his lawyer, everything stopped. A few months later his lawyer sent me a letter informing me that he would no longer represent that doctor. I never heard from them again. Make sure you keep good records to be able to defend yourself in these situations.

I am convinced more than ever that most doctors want your money and don't give a damn if you get healed. Please don't misunderstand me; the good ones, when you find them, are a gift from God and will be everything you ever believed a doctor or healer should be.

Things to Remember:

◆ Use the Internet to find things like the best juicer and to start looking for information about reports and studies. However, be very careful of the reports and studies you find. Anyone can put something on the Net. The library is a good place for information that is a bit more trustworthy.

◆ Good, caring doctors are out there, but you have to be very careful and be willing to look for them. Do not be afraid to fire a doctor for stepping out of line. Remember: Doctors work for you and your wife. You do not work for them. Make sure they understand that from the start and that they are only consultants.

◆ Prior to setting up an appointment with a doctor:
  • Call and get estimated costs for time of visit
  • Get name of person quoting costs, time and date
  • Ask for references
  • Check references and discuss doctor, then set appointment
  • Ask what information the doctor will need you to bring
  • Suggested list to take with you to the appointment:
    • Note pad
    • Notes from previous meetings

- Person to take notes
- Any information the doctor requested
- MOST IMPORTANT: a list of questions you need answered in writing so you don't forget them.
- An open mind so that you can walk out if you feel the need
- File that you should keep:
  - Large, three-ring binder with separators (may take more than one)
  - One section for each doctor or other provider
  - Within each doctor's section, more sections: one each for meetings, bills, referrals.
  - Any and all payments you make, by date.
  - All notes from telephone interviews, visits, etc., by date.
  - All insurance payment reports
◆ I know this seems like a lot of work but it will be worth it to you by the time your cancer battle is over, however it turns out.

CHAPTER 7

A Dream Vacation

◆ ◆ ◆

This is a dream come true.

— Maxine

Maxine and I had been trying to sell our condo at the time the cancer was found and had hoped to use the small profit we would make to purchase her a new truck. She loved trucks and had a small 1991 red Toyota pickup when I met her. "A woman who owns a truck doesn't need a man," she always said. "If a man's going to be around me, it'll be because I want him, not because I need him."

I felt blessed since she always wanted me around. Her little red truck was a workhorse for us. We mistreated that truck the entire time we were working on our cabin. It was crammed full of building materials and pulling a trailer every weekend we went up to our property to work.

The condo sold sometime in February and we had to use most of the money to pay bills. Not enough was left for a truck.

But Maxine wanted to do something that neither of us had ever done before. She had been reading about cruises to the Caribbean and wanted to go. Now I had never even considered going on a cruise and was not in favor of this. What a waste of money! But I agreed to look into the cost and see what we could find.

Maxine wound her arms around me. She looked up at me in that sweet way of hers. "Honey, we don't know what the future is going to bring. I want us to do something that's just for us. Something we can always remember."

I still recall very clearly how beautiful she looked when she did this and how I was unable to say no to her. I am so thankful that she talked me into that trip because to this day I remember every minute of it.

I started looking at different cruises that were available for the end of March or first week in April of that year. It was now February of 2000 and somewhat late to be looking for a trip in March (or at least that's what I was told). I was getting prices of seven to eight thousand dollars for a seven-day cruise. We had that amount of money for the cruise, but I refused to spend that much on a one-week trip, so I continued to check with travel agents.

Finally, about two weeks before we wanted to sail, when it looked like we were not going to be able to go, I happened to call an agency that said they could get us in a mini-suite on The Grand Princess in the last week of March for only six thousand dollars. Well, that sure sounded better; I said, "Maybe," and continued looking elsewhere. A week before the date The Grand Princess was going to sail, the agency called me back and offered the same deal but at forty-two hundred dollars for the seven-day cruise. This cost included the mini-suite with outside balcony, a butler and airfare to Fort Lauderdale and home. No other offer had even come close, so I had to accept this one and we had only one week to get ready to go.

SETTING SAIL

We left Seattle late on a Saturday night, since that was the only flight we could get with such late notice. Flying all night is a real drag, since I happen to be one of those people who is scared to death of flying. I was white-knuckled all the way there and sleep was almost impossible. We got to Fort Lauderdale about seven on Sunday morning and our ship was to set sail at six that evening. Once on board we were exhausted and went to our room to rest. I never told Maxine, but I was hoping that I would not get sick being on this large ship. The last couple times I had gone fishing I had been green and heaving the whole time. Once we were underway, I was pleasantly surprised to find out that the ship was so big you could hardly tell it was on water.

Leaving port was unreal to us. We stood up on the highest deck that we could get to and watched the lights fade in the distance. Within a couple hours we both had fallen in love with cruising and were already talking about where we wanted to go next.

Once we were far enough out to sea that we could no longer see any lights, it was time to look around for something to eat. We had not eaten for about 10 hours because we were either too tired or too excited. The ship had 15 or more places to get food. It was all-you-can-eat and came with the cost of your cruise. That first night we chose the upper deck smorgasbord that must have had at least eight entrees and dozens of fruits, desserts, vegetables, salads, etc. That first meal on board told us that what others had warned us was true: Don't go on a cruise expecting to not gain weight. We stuffed ourselves and then walked around the ship until after midnight. Neither of us wanted to go to our room for fear of missing something.

For the next seven days and nights the cancer was forgotten. We were newlyweds again. It was like a honeymoon that we'd never thought we would have. The only mornings we did not sleep in until 10 or 11 were the ones when we went ashore to go shopping. St. Martins was Maxine's favorite place, I think, in the entire world. For a woman who likes to shop, it is heaven. I only wish I'd had about ten thousand dollars extra so that she could have bought more of the things she wanted. One thing she bought and absolutely adored was a black coral necklace. I believe she loved that necklace more than any other thing I had ever given her. She is wearing it in my favorite picture of her that I carry in my wallet even now.

Game Show

Between our stop in St. Thomas and our next port Maxine and I got tagged to be contestants on a newlywed game that was played on board. With about 30 couples asking to be on it, we were interviewed to see who would be picked. The question they asked us was how we met. When we told them that we had been married less than two years and that we met from a newspaper ad, they chose us.

That night Maxine wore a blue dress that was low cut and short. She did not wear any nylons since she had a perfect tan on her legs and they looked great. She had her long blonde hair fluffed out in what I guess they call "big hair." She looked like a million.

As soon as we sat down, the announcer asked, "Alan, what did you write to get Maxine to answer your newspaper ad?"

I didn't want to go into everything so I said, "Well, I asked for a blue-eyed blonde."

Some guy in the back yelled out, "Way to go Alan!" I was embarrassed, but Maxine was delighted since she loved to be the center of attention. The guys left the room so that the wives could answer questions. When I came back, I was very surprised to discover what my little church girl was willing to say to a crowd of people that we did not even know.

"The question," said the announcer, "was, 'Where was the wildest place you and you husband decided to get loving at?'"

I tried to be very careful of my answer. I never thought for even one second that she would tell them about the outdoor shower, so I didn't get any points for that one.

"What kind of vehicle does Maxine compare you to?"

I thought about it. "It would have to be some kind of truck, because she complains that I never stop working."

The announcer shook his head. "She says you are a Hemi Orange 1969 Plymouth Road Runner with a 440 and four-speed."

Maxine was grinning impishly.

Of course we didn't get any points, but we sure got a lot of hoots from the audience with her answers. In the end we did not win the prize, but we sure met a lot of people that night and we seemed to have put on the best show (or at least Maxine did). It was one of those nights that I will never forget. We had so much fun and she looked so good that a picture of her is burned into my memory forever.

The Naked Truth

The next port we went to was the Island of St. Martens, and we got a bit of a surprise.

"Take us to the most beautiful beach on the island," Maxine told the cab driver. So off we went to Orient Beach. Orient Beach was an incredible place, with great surf and blue water so clear that you could see fish all around you.

The fun part came when we got settled on some beach chairs and Maxine looked at the couple just a little ways from us. She turned to me with a surprised look on her face. "They have no clothes on," she whispered. She had missed the sign that said "Clothing Optional" at the entrance to the beach.

This was more than she could handle, so we moved to another part of the beach where she felt better after looking around. I was laughing so hard at all of this since I could see that about fifty percent of the people walking on the beach and getting settled into chairs were naked. There was nowhere on the beach we could go and get away from the bare bodies. It took her some time to get used to it, but she was determined to enjoy her time on the beach so she tried not to look at anyone for the first couple hours.

Once she was used to the idea of people being naked, she turned to me and said, "Isn't it strange how the people that should never let themselves be seen naked are the ones that walk around that way?"

By the end of the afternoon we had only seen about three or four that could get away with walking around with no clothes and look good doing it. The funny thing is that by now she was taking pictures of them. She wanted to prove to her friends back home that she had gone to a nude beach. Believe me, very few of her friends would have believed it had they not seen pictures of her there. Maxine always liked to wear a bikini, but that's as far as she would go with the nude bit. I, for one, am not so proud of myself that I would ever strip and show off; I don't care if it is a nude beach or not.

The trip was seven days of love and romance between us and we felt like kids playing and having fun. The last day was spent on an island that the Princess Line owned and they provided a barbecue and music. We went snorkeling and had a ball watching many different types of fish swarm around us. I found one of those large conch shells. It was lying on the bottom about fifteen feet down so I swam down to get it. However, when I tried to pick it up I found it to be a lot heaver than I had expected. Well, it was still alive and the animal inside it was big. I took it up so we could look at it and then went back down and deposited it where I found it. I was surprised at how fast it disappeared.

That day was hot and fun and we both got very tanned from being out in the sun all day long. It was a perfect last day for our cruise, but it was also a sad day because the next morning we would be back in port and heading home.

SAD NEWS

It would have been a perfect vacation except for the news on the next to the last evening of our cruise. I received a call from the mainland that my son was trying to reach me. It took a while, but I was finally able to get him on the phone. He informed me that Maxine's stepfather had died. We knew that he was not in very good shape and that it was going to happen soon, but I had been hoping that he would be able to hold on until we got home. I had no choice but to inform Maxine of this and it made the last day a little sadder. She was able to maintain herself after an hour or so of crying and we continued to have a great time, but I know that a good share of the fun had been taken out of it for her. However, our flight home was much better than the flight over, because they had booked us in first class on the way back and we were able to relax.

THINGS TO REMEMBER:

◆ If you and your bride discover anything like cancer, then figure out a way to take her somewhere special alone. I guarantee you will be glad you did if anything happens to her in the future. It may cost some money to do that something extra for your girl, and you may have to give up something else, but it's worth it.

◆ Every naturopath we talked to, as well as some doctors, told us how much mental attitude would mean toward Maxine being able to fight the cancer, so I did all I could to make as many days fun for her as I possibly could.

◆ I have found that watching the film I have of this trip gives me more relief from the pain of losing her than anything else I have done. The joy and happiness we shared back then comes pouring out and it makes me feel great. How wonderful that I had that time and can remember it anytime I want. You will find this to be true also. Looking at the films and pictures will hurt, but it will fill your heart with such love. I know you will have tears falling continuously. It's okay. Let the tears come; it helps.

CHAPTER 8

Going Natural

◆ ◆ ◆

We need more down-to-earth "for real" honesty in this world. Less pretending and sweeping things under the rug would help everyone! How about first and foremost getting honest with God? I believe everything else then has a way of falling into place.

— Maxine

Maxine was totally convinced that going natural in her cancer battle was the only way for her. I talked to her several times about standard medicine, but she had studied a lot of books by then and there was no way to convince her otherwise. After her lumpectomy in January of 2000 Maxine was found to have no sign of cancer. She was determined that she could keep it out by natural means. I started a new job in May of that year, and since she had been declared cancer-free we were able to have medical insurance again. This would be a blessing in the future. We would have health insurance through my work and if I finished working at that job I would still have Cobra coverage. Each day as I was working, Maxine read and studied everything she could find. I would get home to find her wrapped up in another book or report that she had picked up at a bookstore or the library.

A Safe Diet

Because of Dr. Lorraine Day's book, *Cancer Doesn't Scare Me Anymore,* Maxine put herself on a strict diet of vegetables, protein (mostly free range turkey and chicken) and juicing. It was my job to keep juice made for her, so every third day I would spend about an hour standing at the juicer making up four to six pint jars full of either green juice or carrot juice. The green juice was a combination of celery, parsley, cilantro, cucumbers, zucchini squash, spinach, Granny Smith apples and a piece of ginger root. I would mix in some Granny Smith apples and ginger root with the carrot juice also to make it taste better. I had no way to cure her, so I was determined to do everything I could to let her know how much I loved her and wanted her to stick around. I would have stood there and juiced day and night if I thought it was going to help. We even threw out the microwave the first month of 2000 since we read that it changed the molecular structure of the food we put in it; almost every natural food book we read said not to use one.

We found out that going natural means that you must also look at what you did to your body before you started on a "safe diet" (meaning all organic and no chemicals or preservatives). That means you need to detox yourself to get rid of toxins that have been stored in your body for years. I was not going to let Maxine do something alone, so each time she found a detox treatment I did the program along with her. This made for some interesting times and ingesting some foul-tasting herbs that were supposed to clean us out. They must have worked because I will tell you that we got cleaned out, but good. Or so we thought... We would learn in 2001 that we were not as clean as we thought we were.

During 2000, Maxine and I tried to keep to this strict diet; however, we did go out and eat improperly several times a month. Sometimes you just want to eat something that is not classified as a vegetable. Going out and having a steak for me, and salmon for her was very nice once in a while, and for about 10 months after she had been declared cancer-free it appeared we had the cancer under control, if not beaten.

She went in for MRIs, ultrasounds, and had blood drawn for testing every three months. Ever since the lumpectomy in January, 2000, she was on her healthy diet and all tests had been coming back negative. We were excited about the possibility that there may not be any more cancer within her. I was starting to regain hope and Maxine started smiling continuously again. For over a year I had felt as if I was in a losing battle and that anything I did wasn't enough. This is such a miserable feeling for a man and I was now beginning to be rid of it.

One of the benefits of our diet was that not only were we both able to get down to the clothing sizes we always wanted to be, but we felt physically better than we had in years. Maxine had worked very hard to get to a size 8 before "going organic." Now she had made it to a size 8 without even trying. She even got down to a size 6, and did she look good in a short skirt or a bikini! The thrill of being able to buy and wear that size made her extremely happy and the way she looked made me rather happy too. I found it amazing how strong and energized the body could be if fed the right kinds of clean food. If the diet didn't keep the cancer away, at least Maxine would have a very high quality of life while fighting it.

CHANGES

We made it into 2001 doing rather well. I was running my own consulting business and had a very good contract with a large fiber optic company. We had just started working on this new contract and I was letting Maxine be in charge of the entire project for the first time. I had been teaching her how to manage and inspect a construction project for a couple of years. This was to be the first complete project for her. She was so excited about being able to run the job and started out working with great enthusiasm.

Unfortunately, during this time she started feeling like something was wrong in her breast. She was unable to describe it. One day about three weeks into the project she called me and told me that she was worn out and could not finish the day. I came out to the project to take over.

"Alan, I've made an appointment for Thursday with a naturopath in Seattle." Her smile was gone. "I'm scared. Honey, I think the cancer's back."

I was terrified. *Not again*, I was thinking. We'd only had about eight months with no sign of cancer. Now I was literally sick to my stomach.

The naturopath sent us to First Hill Diagnostic for a consultation. We met with Dr. Bruce Porter. Of course I was very much concerned about seeing another new doctor. But Dr. Porter was one of those doctors you pray that you'll find if ever you are sick. He had specialized in breast cancer imagery for most of his 30 years as a doctor and was known all over the world from his lectures on this topic. I will never be able to thank him enough for the loving help he provided us with over the next two years.

The ultrasound did not look good. Three small tumors appeared to be growing along the incision made by the surgeon in the past surgeries. Doctor Porter informed us a biopsy would need to be done. We agreed and set up the appointment. We were never nervous in Dr Porter's office as we had been in other doctor's offices. The concern and love for every patient was obvious from each staff member. It was one of the few places Maxine learned, over time, to feel safe.

The day of the biopsy came and we were there on time and

ready to go. I was going to be in the room with Maxine, since I wanted to hold her hand through every procedure she had to endure. However, the biopsy did not go quite as easily as we had assumed it would.

The doctor had to numb the area of the breast where he was to insert a large needle. We were in there for an hour as he tried time and again to penetrate the first lump. Her body had been able to form a hard shell-like substance around the tumor and he could not get the needle through it. I had to go sit down at one point after about 30 minutes, because I was getting sick watching. I have never done well with needles of any kind. But when Maxine asked where I went, I jumped back up and put my hand on her feet to assure her I was there. My concern for her helped make the sick feeling go away. I was not about to let her go through that without me just because of my weak stomach.

The biopsy proved that our worst nightmare had come back. The tumors were cancer. After the biopsy, Dr. Porter ordered an MRI and that was when even smaller tumors were found along with an involved lymph node.

All my fears returned in a rush: Why her? Why us? What now? At least we'd had insurance for awhile; we were on COBRA. But we knew that it would run out in March of 2002. We believed and hoped we could come up with new insurance by that time.

I found myself sitting outside that night crying alone in the barn. I had told Maxine something lame about going out to look for camping gear. What I did was hide. I believe this was the first time I went to the barn and began pounding my fist into the walls. All the feelings of being useless came back in a flash. I could not believe that this was happening to her. Would I be able to keep my sanity this time? How I wished I could sit down and talk to someone about everything. But I didn't know anyone who'd been through what I was going through and had no clue how to find anyone.

I felt I had to stuff my feelings and get back inside with her and hold her and talk to her about another lumpectomy surgery she was now facing. I knew she was very frightened and I hurt so badly inside I wanted to scream and break something. I was so lost. Trying to stay strong for her took everything I had. I know I had help from Above on this because I don't believe I'm that strong on my own.

Maxine was really into the vegetarian diet by now and was sticking to it, along with juicing every day. There was no cheating on her part at all and I was so proud of how she would turn down anything that was not "good for her."

THE THIRD SURGERY

During this time we started interviewing several surgeons. We wanted to find the right one, who would do exactly what we wanted: no more, no less. Several would not do as we wished and wanted total control of the surgery. This was not acceptable to us, since at this point we had chosen to use doctors as consultants, not to have them completely in charge of our healthcare. Maxine had taken charge of her own care and she meant to keep that responsibility. We finally found a very good surgeon who agreed to our terms. She asked only that we listen so that she could explain her opinion. We listened to her, but Maxine informed her that she was not going to do as the surgeon suggested. We red-lined the permission to treat paper that they always make you sign, and wrote in only what Maxine wanted done. Then Maxine signed each change and made the surgeon sign each change.

The third surgery was to be a removal of about a third of Maxine's right breast. The surgeon wanted to remove the entire breast, but Maxine refused. We had discussed the idea of removing the entire breast, but Maxine was afraid that she would get cancer within the chest wall. I was very nervous about this decision of hers and questioned her several times about it. I was of the feeling that she should have the entire breast removed. This was an inner feeling that I really cannot explain, but it was nagging at me for days as we waited for the surgery date. I told her that I would rather have her lose a breast than to take the chance of losing her.

The surgery went well, however we were told that they were unable to get clean margins. This meant that there was residual cancer within her breast.

Was I right or wrong not to push her about her decision? I believe she would have changed her mind if I had really persisted. I wish I had the answer because it haunts me every day. I wish there had been some way to know which course of action to take. I have to rely on the fact that it was ultimately her choice to make — and I will always defend her choice.

Maxine had now had to endure a third surgery and told me that it was the last one. She felt that she would be unable to go through another one, no matter what may happen. We knew that the cancer was still in her and that we would have to intensify our natural "treatment." At this time we did not know exactly what we would do, but we would read everything on earth if need be to find out. I promised her that I would back her up and commit myself one hundred percent to whatever treatment she chose. It was now May, 2001. She was just turning 48 and still looked as if she was in her 30s. We had only been married for three years.

GETTING HONEST

One afternoon I was so agitated I wanted to climb out of my skin. I'd been picking at Maxine all day and being a real ass.

"That blasted cat of yours just puked in the living room again."

Maxine got a damp cloth and some rug cleaner. "Muffin's just old, honey."

"It's not just old, it's retarded. I swear I'm going to toss that animal out and shoot it."

Maxine gave me a look and took the damp cloth to the laundry room, stepping over a box. But I wasn't done yet.

"When are you going to clean some of this junk out of the house?"

"It's not all junk, honey." She walked into the kitchen.

I followed her and leaned against the fridge. "It is junk. You're gone all day at these yard sales; I get home and see yet another truckload of it. We don't even have room for all the trash you've already brought in."

"I got a lot of organizing done yesterday."

"You got one box dumped out, Maxine, one box. There's a whole bedroom in there that's nothing but boxes."

I could have gone on and on. Maxine always had a calm, cheerful answer. But today she had about had enough. She turned and for the first time I saw the fatigue in her eyes. "Just what in the world do you expect from me?" she said.

And I did not know what to say. I looked at her for a few seconds and broke down crying. "I want you well; I want you free of cancer. I don't understand why this is happening. I don't want you to be sick, Maxine; I'm scared to death of losing you."

She threw her arms around my neck and all I could do was hold her and kiss her and tell her how much I loved her as tears ran down my face. It was the first time she had ever seen me cry. We clung to each other, both of us crying, for about ten minutes. I was holding her so tight that she was hardly able to breathe, but she did not want me to let go.

THINGS TO REMEMBER:

- ◆ I would advise any man to forget your own petty problems and concentrate on hers. Be there for her. I don't care how much you don't like hospitals, needles or whatever. If you love her, be there for her.

- ◆ Something that people may need to know is that you can redline anything you don't like on medical permission sheets and write in what you want. Initial each redline or addition and make the doctor initial them also. And get a copy. Don't let any doctor touch you who says you cannot do that. If they tell you that, find someone else.

- ◆ Let her know early on, and as often as possible, how much you love her, and hold her close every day as if it were the last time you would ever get to do so.

CHAPTER 9

Cost Problems

◆   ◆   ◆

Alan and I have been praying aloud together every night
just before going to sleep. We just decided to bring our
concerns and requests (as well as our thanks) to God —
together. And we have been confessing faith in our desperate
financial situation as well as for my complete healing.

— Maxine

I don't want this to sound like a hard luck story, but the fact is
money does play a large part in a cancer battle. No matter
what type of treatment a person has, the expense is extremely
high. It was difficult for us to afford all of the treatments, testing, food, drugs and supplements that she needed and we
ended up in tremendous debt by the end. But, to be honest, I
never cared about the debt. Anything we had could be sold. We
did whatever was necessary to keep her alive and well.

In the beginning we did not have health insurance. Since
the tumor was found during this time, we could not get cover-

age again until Maxine was declared cancer-free. The first surgery took all of our cash reserves at the time and I had to put almost everything else we were doing on hold. Within two weeks of the first surgery, we received bills from fifteen to twenty different providers. This stripped us of any money we had and left us in a bad way for the second surgery.

When it came time for the first lumpectomy, I was broke as far as cash for the 50% up-front money that they wanted. One of my sons, Chris, came to our rescue. He gave up the college money he'd earned working as a construction laborer so that Maxine could have her surgery. It was no small amount—it was thousands of dollars and it took me two and-a-half years to pay him back. He took the chance of not being able to attend college that next year. You can imagine how I felt when he did that; I was both embarrassed and incredibly proud. How many 20-year-olds could or even would do something like that for their stepmother?

PAYMENT SYSTEM

After this second surgery we were in extreme debt. We now had about 25 providers wanting payments and we had to make up a payment system to be able to give some to each one every month. They did not like the idea that we could not pay everything at once, but had to agree that getting a payment each month was better than getting nothing at all. We kept very close track of these expenses so that we would know where we stood at any time. We had a file for each provider and copies of every bill and payment.

I knew my current job would take care of us very well for almost a year. We were keeping the bills paid and even slowly paying off some of the providers that had been involved in the first two surgeries.

EXPENSE OF NATURAL TREATMENTS

During this time we really were thinking that we might have the cancer beaten. That lasted from January of 2000 to March of 2001, when we found the new tumor. Maxine and I kept working on natural treatments. Now these treatments were not covered by insurance so we had to pay for them ourselves. Anyone who thinks that natural treatments are cheaper than traditional medical ones is fooling himself.

The minerals, vitamins and supplements she was taking cost us several hundred dollars a month. The naturopaths she went to see required payment at the time of the appointment, and that cost hundreds more. All of the testing that we were having done was billed to the insurance company, but we still had a percentage to pay. When you have a number of different providers at the same time, the amounts start to add up very fast.

Once we had the third surgery done in 2001 we had so many doctors, hospitals, laboratories and x-ray techs sending us bills that it amounted to tens of thousands of dollars. All of this on top of the cost of eating only organic was taking everything I could earn along with both of our retirements and savings. We were even forced to sell off items to keep the bills paid. The contract I had was just keeping us above water and did so until the 9/11 terrorist event. Prior to that event, I had several projects lined up to start and everything was looking good. Within two weeks of 9/11, every project I was planning to be working on had its money pulled. In October of 2001, I was out of work and we were trying to keep Maxine's diet going and keep the bills paid with what little savings we still had.

I was out of work and unable to find work; I felt like the most useless person on earth. I tried to keep up my faith, to keep smiling and talking like we would come out in great shape — anything I had to do to keep her from seeing how scared I was.

ASKING FOR HELP

I was so afraid of not being able to provide for her needs that I was looking for any way I could to make money. This is when I got so desperate that I finally had to ask for help. *My ego had finally been beaten.* I should have asked for help a lot sooner, but I thought I could handle anything.

In March of 2002 I had to ask my youngest son, Bryan, by now 20 years old, for a loan of his hard-earned money. He, like Chris, agreed to do it. He loaned enough money to keep Maxine in the treatments she was taking at that time. Once again I had a son willing to loan his dad and stepmother thousands of dollars that he had earned for his college expenses.

How lucky can a man be to have sons like that? I was not as embarrassed this time, but I was just as proud of him as I was of his brother. It took me until March of 2003 to pay him back and during that time he worked extra hours and did whatever he had to do to stay in college.

DEPLETED RESOURCES

By the time Maxine finally went to be with the Lord, we had spent every cent we had for three and a half years on cancer. During the battle we depleted both of our retirement plans, lost our property in Tonasket (on which I figure we lost about $50,000), were unable to pay our income taxes and ended up owing around $75,000 to the IRS.

In the year after Maxine died, I was blessed by being paid a back settlement from the Veterans Administration for a disability I have from my time in the Marine Corps ('71 to '73.) The amount they gave me was around $95,000, of which all but $10,000 went to pay off bills, along with most of what I made working that year. This was hard for me since Maxine and I knew for several years that I would win that award and we had planned on buying her a new truck and putting the rest toward our land and cabin. Until I sat down and wrote this chapter I had not had the nerve to add up all that I still owe due to those three and a half years. Looking at the $265,000 total is somewhat disheartening; however, all I can do is laugh at it. The money seems so trivial considering that I lost the love of my life.

I know that it sounds like a lot of money, especially if you are a working man such as myself, but you cannot allow yourself to be obsessed with it. You have to give everything you have to protect your loved ones and even everything you can borrow or beg. It takes the pride out of you and makes you a more humble man.

The bright spot is that when things seem at their worst you will see the beauty of your fellow men and women. Give up your pride and ask for help and you will be surprised how much help you will receive.

THINGS TO REMEMBER:

◆ Create a file for each provider and copies of every bill and payment. Keep these bills and records in good order so that you can refer to them in the future.

◆ I should have asked for help a lot sooner, but I thought I could handle anything. That was not very smart of me and I hope any man reading this book will be willing to ask for help long before I did.

CHAPTER 10

Intensified Natural Treatment

◆ ◆ ◆

Yesterday at PCC Market in Issaquah I was asked by the checker, "Christina" if I would like to make a donation for breast cancer research. I said, pleasantly, "No, thank you. I have breast cancer and I'm fighting it naturally. I don't believe in their typical AMA program of looking for the answer with chemotherapy and radiation." With that we struck up a conversation. All the while she was ringing up my $105 worth of organic/health-building groceries. (I wish someone would start a fund for "Natural Cancer-Beating-Wallet-Depleted Families!") When I was finished paying, Christina walked all the way around the counter to give me a hug — even though they were quite busy. Such kindness is a rare and beautiful thing in our world today. May I pass it along to another — soon!

— Maxine

Maxine had had the last surgery she was going to have, as far as she was concerned. She knew she still had cancer within her breast and was determined to beat it by the only method we had at our disposal. She looked for and found a naturopath who would work for her and she proceeded with an even more strenuous natural regime.

This meant considerably more money being spent on these natural treatments, which no insurance would ever cover. We simply had to come up with the money, even if it meant giving up everything we owned.

BUILDING THE IMMUNE SYSTEM

Maxine was taking a number of all-natural minerals and supplements and began drinking a tea called "Essiac" after reading *The Essiac Report* by Richard Thomas. *"The results we obtained with thousands of patients of various races, sexes and ages, with all types of cancer definitely proves Essiac to be a cure for cancer. Studies done in laboratories in the United States and Canada also fortify this claim,"* Dr. Charles A. Brusch M.D. *(endorsement of front cover of book.)*

It was a good-tasting tea and it really helped her calm down and sleep better at night. Whether it really helped kill the cancer within her is unknown. Maybe it did slow it down, but I have no way of saying one way or another. Sleep is supposed to be very good for cancer patients. Without the tea she was lucky to get three hours sleep a night; she would wake up several times. Many nights she would leave the bed and go downstairs to read, unable to get back to sleep. I knew this was not a good sign but I could do little about it.

The juicing that she started considerably earlier, along with its cost, was intensified and she was drinking eight 8-oz. glasses of fresh organic juice each day, along with eating only vegetarian foods. She also started going to a clinic in Tacoma to have her blood checked. She studied books on meditation and how to completely calm herself so that her body would not have to work on too many things at once. The calming allowed her immune system to concentrate on the cancer. Or at least that's what I was told about all of these things. To be truthful I was ready to try anything, so long as it was natural and there was no threat to it.

DENTAL DETOX

Maxine finished reading a book titled *Uninformed Consent,* an in-depth study on dental toxicity. The authors, (Hal A. Huggins, D.D.S., M.S. and Thomas E. Levy, M.D., J.D.) explained the dangers of having mercury amalgams and root canals in your mouth. A large percentage of amalgams are made up of mercury and everyone knows how deadly mercury is. He also explains about the infections that are always at the base of a root canal and advises people to have all root canals removed from their mouths. After reading about these possible problems Maxine decided to have all of her amalgam fillings along with any root canals removed from her mouth.

We wanted to make sure her dental work was done safely, so I contacted Dr. Huggins' office and asked if there were any dentists in the Northwest that had trained in the methods of safe removal he explained in his book. We were happy to find out there were, in fact, a couple in Washington State. The one we chose is in Shoreline, WA.

Maxine's first appointment turned out to be a shock; the cost of her treatment was going to be around fifteen thousand dollars. The plan was to complete her work one quadrant at a time with several weeks between each appointment to allow for her to recover. Unfortunately the insurance we had covered less than ten percent of the work needed. I was working at the time, so Maxine proceeded to have the work done while I budgeted for each appointment. The dental office knew we were on a tight budget and did all they could to help us out.

Maxine wanted to have her one root canal removed because she was getting some pain in the general area, and she believed what the book had told her about root canals being dangerous. When the dentist removed the tooth, he found a hole at the bottom of the root that was filled with infection. There is no way to tell how long the infection had been in her jaw, but when the tooth came out it made the entire room stink. It was exactly as the book had described it would be. Up to that point I was a bit unconvinced that we needed to spend so much money for dental work. After seeing that infected root canal I agreed with her one hundred percent and wanted everything done by the book.

Maxine's dental work took about six months to complete due to the recovery times she needed between appointments. After each appointment I would take her to her chiropractor to be checked and adjusted. Natural medicine explains that the jaw and neck get out of place when dental work is done. It is recommended that after a dental appointment everyone should get adjusted. With Maxine having cancer we took no chances and she was checked after every dental procedure.

Between the dental and the chiropractic, she was completely exhausted by the time we got home and needed to take a nap. I always tried to make sure she did not have to do anything other than rest on those days. That meant I was cooking dinner and making sure everything was taken care of at home.

OZONE COLONIC

I was somewhat surprised one day when she told me she was going to have a treatment called an ozone colonic. Now I knew what a colonic was but I had never heard of an ozone colonic and I was very apprehensive. My first reaction was to say "no" because of the cost, which had to be paid at the time of each treatment. I told her that we did not have the money for them. She refused to believe that, and proceeded to inventory what else we could do without so that she could pay for the colonics. Because of my concern, I not only took her to that appointment but also insisted that I take the treatment so I would know what she was getting into. It turned out that it was not as scary as we thought at first and it did help her considerably. We learned that it would take about fifteen treatments to clean out her liver completely, along with her colon. The best time for us to do these treatments was on Sunday after church. Each Sunday afternoon we would drive the sixty miles to the office and she would have her treatment and then we would drive home and she would have to lie down and rest. These treatments did leave her exhausted.

What we found very surprising was the presence of Candida, a fungus, (see *The Yeast Connection* by William G. Crook, MD) in her body. The ozone would cause the Candida to die and the adhesions where it lived within the colon would come loose and be eliminated. Now Maxine was only five feet, five inches tall and weighed about 130 pounds at that time; on her 11th treatment we saw an adhesion approximately two feet long come out of her. That adhesion alone had billions of Candida cells on it that were now dead and leaving her body. She really felt better after that appointment and continued to feel better each time we went there for additional treatments.

We were also surprised to find out that most women have a lot of Candida within them and it lives and grows on things like sugar and anything sweet. Only a very strict detox can kill this fungus and eliminate it from the body. Men aren't bothered with it anywhere near as much as women are. From what we learned, I believe every woman should study Candida and consider ways to eliminate it from her body.

There are a number of good publications on Candida listed in the back of this book.

Don't ever think that these treatments are cheap because they are not. We had to pay for them as we went, so each week for about 15 weeks I had to come up with a sizable amount of money. At first I was not sure if it was worth it, but as the treatments progressed I saw a considerable change in Maxine's energy level. Once she got over the fatigue of the treatment she seemed to have a lot more energy and feel much better. I was not going to argue with that, so I never said anything and we proceeded on with them. I even decided to have a couple more treatments myself. I had found from my first treatment that I had stored chemicals within my body that had most likely been there my entire life. That first treatment had shown this and it really bothered me that I had that stuff inside of me. After two more treatments I was clean of the chemicals, or at least we did not get any indication that I had any more in me. I was quite glad about that and felt better than I had for many years. I will be having more of these treatments every so often in the future just to make sure I'm not a storehouse for more toxic chemicals.

RIFE MACHINE

Another cancer treatment that Maxine had been reading about had to do with radio frequencies. Thank God this one did not cost us anything since the people who provided the equipment simply wanted persons with cancer to try their system in hopes of finding the right frequencies.

The story is that a man in the 1920s by the name of Royal Rife had developed a method of killing cancer cells by duplicating their frequencies and causing the cell to be destroyed (see RoyalRife.com) As the story goes, Rife claimed that he could cure cancer patients and wanted to show the medical community. He was given 12 terminal patients somewhere near San Diego who were considered to have less than a month to live. Rife used his frequencies on each of these people and within a month each patient was completely cured of the cancer (or so the story goes.) You can see a picture on the Internet of a large gathering where doctors all over the country held a huge banquet in honor of Royal Rife as the man who cured cancer.

Claim was that the president of the AMA (or whatever they called it back then) wanted to buy the rights to Rife's system so that medical doctors could control it and charge for the use of it. Rife did not want to do that because his plan was to give his work away free to help everyone who had cancer. The story continues to tell how Rife's refusal brought about the destruction of his work. Once it was known to the president of the AMA that Rife intended to give his cure away free, the "powers that be" set up a situation whereby Rife's laboratory was ransacked and his work destroyed by what were claimed to be government agents. He had to run to Mexico to escape being put in jail. I don't know just how much of this story is true or embellished. However, I do know that there are a lot of people all around this country trying to copy Rife's work with the frequencies and they are doing it very secretly. It took Maxine and I some time to locate one of these people.

We were surprised at how nervous the man was who let us use his equipment to treat Maxine. He would only allow me a cell phone number and never gave me his address. I don't even know what city he lives in. Many had been working on the exact frequency that would kill cancer but none had found it yet. Royal Rife was said to have documented exactly what frequencies would kill over 1000 different viruses. It is unknown to me if anyone has been able to duplicate his work yet. With his notes and equipment having been destroyed, maybe no one will ever be able to do it again.

Anyway, we did get the equipment and each day we tried the frequencies on her breast and on a lymph node in her chest on her right side, which was now infected and growing. Each time we hit certain frequencies she said that the tumor would vibrate or jump. We know that the cancer did not like being bombarded with these frequencies; however we were unable to find just the right one to destroy the cancer. We tried this for two or three months. We finally gave up when she got discouraged with it. Nowadays there are ads on the radio about doctors using radio frequencies for several different ailments. Could this mean that the story of Royal Rife's work is true?

NATURAL BENEFITS

Our natural battle did not stop here. Maxine continued to read and search for diets and supplements that would be beneficial to her battle: pure water, lots of rest, wheat grass juice (see *Wheat Grass, Nature's Finest Medicine* by Steve Meyerowitz), relaxation, lowering stress as much as possible, gallons of pure organic juice, anything we could find to help promote the health of her immune system.

I believe that all these things we did helped keep her alive for a couple years longer than the doctor first believed she would live. Up until the day she had to take radiation for the cancer that had spread into her brain, no one could ever tell she had cancer or anything else. She looked that healthy. From following these diets I also found myself feeling better than I had ever felt before and I've been a health nut for most of my life.

THINGS TO REMEMBER:

- ◆ I would advise anyone to read the book *Uninformed Consent* and draw your own conclusions about how serious dental work is. There's another book titled *Dental Mercury Detox* that you might want to read too.
- ◆ You may find yourself doing laundry, scrubbing floors, cooking meals, cleaning house and a million other things that you cannot let her do when she is fighting for her life.
- ◆ I would advise you to talk to a naturopath and get on a clean diet along with your wife. It will help give you the

strength to carry on with the many chores you will find yourself having to do to help her. Even if she uses chemo and radiation it will help her immune system recover.

◆ Do not give up completely on standard medicine. Keep having regular checkups and blood tests every three months, just in case something comes up. I would advise you to study both natural and standard medicine journals for new developments. Also, find one doctor you trust who will keep you informed. Don't be afraid to go through several doctors to find the one. Remember, they work for you.

CHAPTER 11

Relatives, Church and Friends

◆　◆　◆

*I have been doing some intense soul-searching. In so
doing, it occurred to me to begin asking Jesus to "heal my
life" not just continually asking Him to heal my body!
I am beginning to understand that in order to live, I need
to be healed — body, soul and spirit. There is so much to
live for! There is so much ahead that I don't want to miss.*
— Maxine

This may be the most difficult chapter for me to write. I'm
not even sure if I should write about relatives since every
one of them is so different and dealt with Maxine's cancer in
individual ways. I will limit myself on this one so as not to
cause any more pain than has already been suffered by the loss
of Maxine.

I wish I could give you some good advice on how to get
through this part, but I'm not sure I got through it well. I would
bet anyone could have done a better job than I did.

FEELINGS OF ABANDONMENT

I unfortunately had the task of listening to Maxine cry herself to sleep a hundred times in the three and a half years we were fighting cancer because of her feeling of having been abandoned by relatives. She would lie in bed in tears praying to God, "Why do I have to be so alone in this battle?"

All I could do was hold her and tell her, "I love you. We'll make it day by day, Max. You're stronger than you think you are. That's what the Bible says, right?"

Every time this happened it felt like my heart was being ripped in two. She was like a small child wanting to be held by her mommy and told that everything would be all right. The problem was that she knew it wasn't all right and chances were that it never would be again.

Sometimes I would get so hurt by this that I would cry with her — not for the same reason, though. I would cry because of my helplessness. Then, later, I would be back in the barn fighting the ghosts since I could not hit anything in front of Maxine. What a sight I must have been punching the walls of that old barn and crying and praying all at the same time.

I must say that my feeling of being useless for not making enough money to support her treatments was very hard on me. This is guilt that I believe I will carry for the rest of my life. Everyone tells me not to blame myself, but to this day I have not found a way to eliminate it from my mind.

One evening when we were very broke, Maxine and I were

trying to come up with a thousand dollars to continue the natural treatments that she was having. We had depleted everything we could think of and were at a loss. With no other solutions in sight, Maxine made a call to a family member. Maybe she would be willing to loan the money.

When Maxine got off the phone, she was crying.

"Tell me what happened," I touched her wet face. "What did she tell you?"

Maxine sat down. "She can't support something she doesn't believe in."

"That's what she told you?"

Her shoulders sagged. "I know she doesn't like alternative medicine but…I thought at least she'd believe in me." Her eyes had lost their shine. "I'm going to go lie down, okay?"

I'd never seen her so devastated. Would she give up hope? I was scared and I was furious. I wracked my brain for options, but could think of nothing. "What now, God?" I prayed. "Is *this* what you want? Is it?"

A VERY NICE SURPRISE

Three hours later the phone rang.

"Alan!" It was my older brother Guy, who was 100% disabled from numerous wounds he received in Viet Nam.

I didn't even want to tell him what kind of day we were having. He'd already been so supportive, giving us a $4,000 loan just two months before. I tried to sound upbeat. "Hey!" I said.

Maxine wandered in and I mouthed his name to her. She grinned, always cheerful with others, even when she was miserable. "Hi Guy!" she called.

"So, Alan, I got a very nice surprise from the VA today."

"Yeah?" I was glad for him. He and his wife, Nola, lived on a pension and certainly were not rich.

"Yeah, and I got the feeling you needed some help. We're overnighting you a check for $1,000."

I was speechless. Guy didn't really believe in the natural treatments we were using for Maxine. And he'd already been generous. I managed a "thank you" before hanging up the phone.

Maxine grabbed me and held on tight, crying, "Thank you, God! Oh, God bless your brother, God bless him!"

It took me a year or better to be able to pay Guy back. Between my brothers and sisters and sons they loaned us approximately $50,000 over the years to keep the battle going. I have now paid back all of them. What a blessing they all were.

SEVEN RESPONSES

If you and your wife are fighting cancer, you will have relatives who react in the following ways:

1. *I agree completely with what you are doing.* This is great but don't expect to find very many of these. They also will help whenever asked, and even at times when you don't ask. These will be your volunteers.

2. *I will back anything you do even if I don't agree with what you are doing.* This is a Godsend for you and there will be little or no trouble with this type. They will help you if you ask them.

3. *I can't bear to think of her having cancer so I am going to distance myself from her completely and only write once in a while.*

4. *I disagree with what she is doing and I will neither offer nor give any support of any kind.* Hard to believe, but I guarantee you will have it happen. If you don't, be very thankful.

5. *I don't know what to do, so I will make like she does not exist and never call or write or even acknowledge her.* Believe it or not, this will happen

6. *I am blind to the entire thing and will treat you like you are perfectly well and that you should be able to do anything anyone else can do with no complaint at all.* Maxine was actually criticized for being tired and having to take a couple naps each day as the cancer got worse.

7. *I think you should be in a hospital all the time under a doctor's care, and I will treat you like an invalid.*

I'm sure that there will be other types you will encounter, however most can be placed within one of the seven categories I have listed.

CHURCH

It was March of 1999 and prior to finding the cancer when Maxine and I found New Community Church in Maple Valley,

Washington. We decided on the first morning we attended that it would be our church from then on. The only reason we went is because one of the members worked with me, and for months kept bugging me to go since he knew we were looking for a church. One Sunday morning I woke up and asked Maxine if she would go to that church just once with me to get him to quit bothering me about it.

We were hooked the first day; Maxine loved the music and we both liked the pastor who came across as a real person in love with the Bible and Jesus (which was just how Maxine was.) I was a new Christian and still was somewhat uncomfortable going to church, since I had not been in a church for over 30 years prior to meeting Maxine. Yet, somehow even I was very comfortable at New Community from the first day. It was now our church and has been my church ever since. I never knew any group of people could or would be so close to me and be of such support as the people at New Community have been. I can openly say I love everyone at New Community and would do just about anything I could for them.

FRIENDS

Maxine was the first person I had ever met that really lived as she spoke and believed. I had met a number of so-called Christians in my life and every one of them would tell you how good a Christian they were just as they were sticking a knife in your back. Maxine was a very smart woman and started me out slowly — getting me to go to church and introducing just a few people that she had known for many years.

As time passed she introduced me to more and more Christians who walked the talk. Now these were people who did not just read the Bible and believe in Jesus, but actually lived their lives in the manner in which they believed. What a joy it was for me to meet people like this.

On September 24, 2001, which was my 50th birthday, we were sitting at home and a car came into our driveway. I looked out the window and asked Maxine, "Who are those people?"

Well, Maxine had set up a little surprise birthday party for me and had invited some people she wanted me to meet. She knew I did not like surprises, especially if it meant meeting new people. She insisted that I would like them and that she thought I would get along well with her friend's husband. That night I met Dr. Terry Newby. I had met his wife Susan before when Maxine had the women over to the house for a prayer meeting, but this was the first time I met Terry.

To my surprise, and delight, Terry and Susan have been my best friends and are so dear to me now that I would be almost lost without them. Their support has been a big part of my being able to cope with the loss of "my girl." They were always there for Maxine and me. When things got really bad, Terry would slip me a hundred dollar bill or Susan would give the same to Maxine. If Maxine was having a bad night she would call them in the middle of the night and they would pray for her. Susan is a mighty prayer warrior and Maxine loved hearing her pray. Every time Susan prayed for Maxine, she got renewed strength and was able to do better almost instantly.

Another couple, Rick and Kathy Parton, become very close to us and Kathy became Maxine's partner in fighting breast cancer. You see, Kathy had already been fighting breast cancer for a couple of years when I first met her and Rick. Maxine had known them for more than twenty years. She and Maxine started trading information since both were fighting the cancer naturally. They had both learned a lot prior to getting together, but now they were sharing information and they were both studying different approaches. They got together often to compare notes and exchange information.

Rick and Kathy were another couple we could always count on when help was needed desperately. Rick was a Master Herbalist and he and Kathy sold all-natural supplements and would sell Maxine supplements at wholesale price or without asking for payment. They even gave her money at times when we needed it. I wish there was some way I could repay the help and kindness that they gave so unselfishly throughout our battle.

Maxine's prayer group, consisting of Maxine, Susan and Janet, would meet once a week at one of their houses and spend an hour or two in prayer for Maxine's life. These were two of her best friends. Maxine and Janet had gone to Bible school and lived together when they were about 20 years old. You could not ask for better people to have around in a health challenge.

If prayer alone could cure cancer or anything else, these three women could save the entire world. There were times when I would see such a difference in Maxine after one of their meetings that I almost began to believe in faith healing. However, this is one area that I have not been able to fully believe in. I have never seen anyone truly healed by "spiritual healing."

POINT MAN MINISTRIES

Terry introduced me to Point Man Ministries. I had never heard of it though it had been around since 1985. It's a Christian veterans' ministry that helps all vets of any service or time. Terry was a member and told me I should go to a meeting with him one Wednesday night. When I asked him what it was all about, he said it was veterans helping veterans. He gave me a book called *Nam Vet: Making Peace with Your Past* by a man named Chuck Dean.

Chuck Dean was the man responsible for running Point Man all over the country and he lived in Seattle. I read *Nam Vet* in one day and was so impressed with what it had to say that I had to go to a meeting. I contacted Terry and he said he would pick me up about 6:00 PM.

That Wednesday I met a band of guys that came from all services and wars. They were in World War II, Korea, Viet Nam, Somalia, Panama, and other operations that they were still not allowed to talk about. They all had one thing in common: the difficultly of trying to live in a world where most people had no idea what they had experienced and what was going on in their heads. Now, I had never been to Nam even though I was in the Marine Corps during that war. I had orders, but they were stopped and I never got there. All of the guys I was in with ended up over there at one time or another and some never made it home. This has been a problem for me for a long time, but I never knew what it was.

The guys at Point Man were quick to point out that I had what they called "survivors guilt." In other words, why did I get lucky and my buddies didn't? I had never thought of it that way before, but they were absolutely right. I had felt guilty for not going over with them and it had been eating at me for 30 years. These guys in Point Man have become brothers to me now and they prayed and were right there for me every minute Maxine and I were in the battle for her life. Many of them came to her memorial and I sure was glad to see them there. I would encourage any and all veterans to look into a local chapter of Point Man or at least read *Nam Vet*. Most vets feel like they are alone and that no one knows what is going on inside them. They also feel like they are the only one thinking the thoughts that they have. It's not true; all vets have these thoughts but few find a place to let them out. Point Man provides that place.

I was constantly feeling this loneliness throughout our cancer battle. Many times I wished that I had a group like Point Man, but with husbands who had been through the cancer battle that I could have talked to.

THINGS TO REMEMBER:

◆ Blaming yourself for lack of money is very tough and I have found the only help is to talk to others about it. Don't try to keep it all inside, because it will eat you up.

◆ If you love her you are going to feel very upset sometimes to the point of wanting to break things. Get yourself someplace where you can do just that without hurting anything of value. Sometimes you will have to let off the steam so you won't burn out.

◆ You must keep believing that the help you need will be there and don't let her see you look discouraged. Remember, you are her number one cheerleader and support. If she sees you looking defeated, it will only cause her to be depressed and that encourages the cancer growth.

CHAPTER 12

Our Last Fun Trip

❖ ❖ ❖

I thank God that I'm able to do these things. I also told
Him I know Heaven will be this wonderful and so much
more — infinitely better, even! I'm just not ready to go yet.
— Maxine

In October of 2001 Maxine and I took what was to be our last
long fun trip together. She was hurting from an infected
lymph node in the upper right portion of her chest, but it was
not too much of a problem at the time. She wanted to go to a
wedding in October in San Diego. We were very short on
money, but we did have enough to go on. That, along with our
credit cards, would allow us to make the trip.

ENJOYING EACH OTHER

We belong to a time share system called Trend West that we
had purchased in the first year we were married. I set us up to
spend a week in Palm Springs after the wedding so that we

could relax in the sun and get rested and tanned. I took the time to do what any good engineer would do: I planned the entire trip hour by hour, day by day, so that we could be orderly as we traveled.

Well, that's not how Maxine did things — once on the road, out went my plans. We left Kent six hours late and drove to the Oregon Coast the first day. We didn't get as far as I had planned but I was satisfied that we could catch up the next day, so we found and stayed in a nice hotel on the beach.

To my dismay the next day we were not able to get more than a mile along the coast highway without seeing something we wanted to stop and look at. We stopped at every tourist trap, park and playground. This went on for the first three days.

Really, we were having a ball. Maxine had hardly said anything about the cancer hurting her and she was happy and laughing and talking to everyone we came across. I finally realized if we were going to get to the wedding before it was over we were going to have to get moving.

Personally, I was having so much fun with Maxine that I didn't care if we ever got there. She, on the other hand, suddenly got worried that we would not make it, so she insisted we cut over to I-5 in San Francisco and head south as fast as our little truck could go. Of course we were still in Oregon and she did not realize how far we had to go. The next 19 hours were spent in the truck driving and only stopping to eat and get gas. We didn't stop for anything else until we got to our room in San

Diego. The wedding was the next day and we were both so worn out from driving that we almost overslept the next morning.

The wedding was beautiful and over far too quickly. Maxine was very happy to have been there. By that night she was hurting and ready for some rest so I went out and got dinner and brought it back. The next morning we headed for Palm Springs and spent five wonderful days swimming and relaxing in the sun.

Maxine wanted me to ride the aerial tramway that goes up to a restaurant on the top of the mountains. I have a hard enough time flying so the idea of riding something that looks like a good breeze could blow it over was not for me. Also, I'm one of those people who cannot tolerate heights. So she decided to ride up by herself to see the view from the mountains. She came down all excited about it and I wished I had gone with her. In the evenings we ate at some nice restaurants and during the day she was shopping or by the pool. The Trend West resort there in Palm Springs is a beautiful place and the staff was great. We couldn't have asked for a better place to stay.

On our last day in Palm Springs I called Trend West to see if I could set up some places to stay on our trip home. Of all things I was able to get rooms at Clear Lake, California and at Klamath Falls, Oregon.

We had decided that we would drive up through the Napa Valley to go home instead of the long dry trip up I-5. It was a beautiful drive. We saw mountains, streams, valleys and some most unusual rock formations. Maxine insisted that we stop every so often so she could pick up a rock to take home. I now have a stack of multicolored rocks from all over the West Coast out on my back porch and I just cannot bring myself to get rid of them.

Near San Francisco we stayed with friends of Maxine and had a great time. Maxine wanted to go with her friend and talk and do woman things, so I said I would hang around the house and relax and try to find something to do. They were gone almost all day and by the time they got back I had juiced a bunch of vegetables for Maxine, since I figured she was going to be worn out and would need the energy they provide. I was right and she was very happy that I would think of that for her.

What a ball we ended up having that night at dinner. To my surprise, all of our hosts' kids showed up with their friends and spouses. It was loud and funny and absolutely a blast. To see a family having that much fun and no one getting upset with anyone was really fun for us. This was the kind of thing Maxine and I enjoyed at our house when all five of our kids were there along with the grandkids. We made plans to get together with her friends again in the future but unfortunately that would never happen.

We drove out the next morning and it seemed like a short trip to Clear Lake simply because we were so well-rested and did not have to hurry at all. Our condo at Clear Lake was like all the other Trend West rooms we had been in. It had a full kitchen so we were able to cook, and a beautiful view of the lake. Clear Lake was a very quiet and peaceful place; however it lacked a good place to eat so we ended up buying hamburgers at a little shop down the road. This is not the type of food a cancer patient should be eating, but we did not have any choice that night. We figured one night would be okay.

That evening it was very calm and we watched the ducks and other birds walk around outside our glass door. We rented a movie that night and just relaxed and enjoyed each other and had a wonderful, peaceful night.

MAXINE MADE FRIENDS WITH THE WHOLE WORLD

We had to leave the next morning so I was up early and got everything ready and let her sleep in. I went to the little shop and got myself a cup of coffee and walked out on the dock just enjoying the fresh, clean morning air. A man and his wife were fishing on the end of the dock. Their little boy was jumping up and down very excited about what his mom had on her line. She appeared to be getting tired. I must have been watching for about a half hour when they finally pulled up a catfish that was at least three feet long and about ten pounds.

I know that a catfish may not excite many people, but when my sons were young we used to go out in the evening and fish for catfish in the Yakima River a half-mile from our home in Richland, Washington. We found them to make very good fish and chips.

I took some photos and talked to the couple for a while and

then went to see if Maxine was up yet. Maxine was more interested in the people than the fish, and had their names, phone numbers and address in her book so that she could write to them in the future. I believe she had that information on every person she ever met. She insisted that I get several pictures of the couple and their son with the catfish.

THE ROAD HOME

Within a couple hours we were on the road again and headed for Klamath Falls, Oregon where we were going to stay at the Running Y Resort. When we got there we found the best room we had ever stayed in. It was more like a townhouse than a room and was beautifully furnished with two bedrooms and a full kitchen that made you feel at home. Maxine made me get out the video camera and record every room in it so that we could show our friends that had asked us about Trend West. I believe that film has caused several of our friends to look into the Trend West system.

There was a restaurant in the resort that served one of the best steaks I have ever had. Maxine had salmon that she said seemed like it was caught that day, it was so fresh. We sat and ate and drank a couple glasses of wine and had a ball talking to the restaurant staff and other people there. Everyone was friendly and wanted to know where we were from. Maxine, in her normal way, got the names and addresses of several people and, sure enough, she sent them cards later.

Early the next morning we were on our way on the last leg of our trip home. She wanted to take a side trip to the top of Crater Lake in Oregon. What an incredible place that is. To think something could explode enough to create a crater that large.

Our trip was almost over, and I should have been happy to be heading back, but for some reason I was getting a bad feeling and I didn't like it. I felt like I didn't ever want to go home and stop this wonderful time we were spending with each other.

Crater Lake was to be our last stop, and we knew once we were home everything would go back to the normal grind of fighting the cancer. Somehow I sensed that this was to be our last real trip together and that everything else from then on would be less than fun. I could feel it but I didn't want to accept it and kept trying to hide from the feeling. I'm glad I didn't know how correct I would be.

CHAPTER 13

The Healing Rooms

◆　◆　◆

God called me up this morning at 7:30 AM —
on the phone! Well, not God Himself, actually…
but He may as well have!!
— Maxine

Maxine had been a believer in faith healing for a long time. She had graduated from Bible college when she was in her early twenties. She believed that the laying on of hands by some people could and would cure illnesses and all during our cancer battle she would have me take her to these different churches and faith healers for help. I went along with this for a year or two because it made her happy. You see, although she had gotten me to become a Christian I still was not, and am not today, a real believer in faith healing.

After a while I noticed that she would get prayed for by these healers and for a couple days she would be looking and feeling better. I believe this was due to her own belief in the healing, because after a few days she would realize that the cancer was still there and growing and she would go into a week of depression. These depressions were hard on her and me also, because she would look like she was ready to give up. I never wanted her to give up so I started refusing to take her to these men or women because I knew what would happen the next week. This is where I was mentally on faith healing when she heard about The Healing Rooms.

JOHN G. LAKE

In the early 1900s there was a pastor in Spokane, John G. Lake, who had a ministry called The Healing Rooms. This was a place where people would come and the pastor would lay hands on the person and pray. Lake had a large following due to some miraculous healings said to have taken place under his hand. People would come to Spokane from all over the West Coast to be healed by this man. These healing rooms stayed open for a considerable time.

The story of John G. Lake is very interesting and I would recommend obtaining a book about his life. This man gave up a great deal back East to come out West and build his ministry. Did he really heal people? I have a hard time believing that, but a lot of people believe he did. I leave it up to you to decide for yourself.

SPOKANE

Maxine had heard that someone had opened The Healing Rooms in Spokane and was praying for people daily. She asked me to take her there but again we were broke, as it seemed like we always were, even when I was working and making good money. The cancer treatments had created so many bills that I could not make enough to keep them covered. Maxine wanted to go to Spokane and she was sure that the Healing Rooms would help her. I tried to explain to her that the 300-mile drive along with hotel costs and food made it impossible for us to go. She fully believed the stories she had been reading and hearing about the faith healers, and she also believed we would find a way to go. To our surprise Maxine got her wish when Terry and Susan Newby paid for our gas, the hotel, and the cost of a seminar.

It was spring of 2002 when we drove over to Spokane with great hopes that maybe, just maybe, something miraculous would happen while we were there. We checked into our room and relaxed that night and tried to get some sleep. This did not work since the City of Spokane was hosting some sort of high school sporting event and the hotel was full of what seemed to be unchaperoned kids.

At 11:00 PM the noise was unreal: kids running up and down the halls screaming and banging on the walls. I had finally had enough and went out after them and was not nice at all about it. I threatened to beat some of them along with a couple coaches who were not controlling the kids. It got really quiet after that.

Then, at about midnight, we were awakened when three men came knocking on our door and introduced themselves as security for the hotel. Someone had claimed that I had threatened him or her. I informed these men (actually kids themselves) that I had merely explained the law of physics: For every action there is an opposite and equal reaction. The reaction was going to be produced by me.

They agreed to keep watch on the kids and I informed them that I was going to file a complaint with management in the morning about them waking us at midnight. They left and the next morning, after talking to the hotel manager, we were given a larger, nicer room in another area away from the kids and noise. The manager was very sympathetic to Maxine's need for sleep and did not want her to have any more problems in his hotel. Once we moved to the new room we were able to get some rest.

Our appointment at the healing rooms was for 3:00 PM. We arrived and filled out a couple of papers and sat down to wait. Maxine was so filled with hope and faith. She truly believed that she was going to be healed and that we would see a miracle happen that afternoon. She was so excited about it that she even got me to dare to hope that something would happen.

We only had to wait a short time when a very sweet lady came and directed us back into a private room. Then a man and his wife walked in and Maxine somehow knew them. Apparently she had read about these two in some book she had at home. They were missionaries and had a reputation for healing. They would be the ones praying for Maxine that afternoon. "Relax," they told her. "Let yourself go and try not to think of anything. Let us do the work of praying."

As they were praying I sat and watched. For once in my life I felt very comfortable with the idea of faith healing — even enthused. What a story we would have to tell if she was cured of cancer and only God would get the glory for the healing.

The prayer went on for almost an hour and by the time we were ready to leave Maxine was looking so much better than when we arrived I could hardly believe it was the same woman. Dared I hope that something had really happened in that hour? It sure looked like it had. Every part of my heart and soul was hoping and praying that I would see a miracle that day.

We got back to our room and prepared to go to a Christian meeting in one of the banquet rooms of the hotel. I had never been to something like this and I could see that Maxine was a little nervous about it. When we got there we found that the pastor in charge of the healing rooms was hosting this meeting and I thought that this might be fun although I had no idea what it was going to be about.

Maxine knew, but she chose not to tell me because she knew if she did I would never have walked into the place. We went inside and sat down. A band was playing some nice

Christian music and people were sitting around talking. It was very pleasant to begin with. After a while the music stopped and The Healing Rooms pastor spoke for a few minutes. When he was done, he said that we would have about twenty minutes of music before starting the meeting, so enjoy. I thought, *Okay, this seems to be rather nice.*

Did I get a surprise. The music came on loud; most of those sitting in the room jumped up and started running around, swinging flags, dancing, shouting and carrying on like a bunch of wild people. The look on my face must have told the story because Maxine said, "This is too much for you, isn't it?"

The look in my eyes answered her question, because after five minutes of this craziness, she smiled and said, "I won't make you sit through this; let's go."

It didn't take me long to hit the door, with her laughing at me all the way back to the room. We spent the rest of the night at a wonderful restaurant having a great Italian dinner. It turned out to be a beautiful night on the town with my gorgeous blonde. However, no more Christian meetings like that one for me.

The next morning we packed up and headed home. She was still feeling great and looked like her old self again. Wow, could it be? At this point I was praying that all of my doubts and nonbelief in faith healing would be shown to be wrong. Oh God, was I ever praying for that.

Unfortunately we would realize all too soon that the miracle did not happen and the tumor was still growing. This really put a strain on my faith, but it never even budged hers.

Yes, she went into a depression for a while, but never gave up on her faith that Jesus was going to heal her and that this was just a trial she had to go through. She would not let me say anything that came remotely close to doubting that God would heal her. If I started to get frustrated and say something negative, she would put her hand on my mouth and say in her sweet way, "Jesus is with us, and He will choose the time for my healing."

Even today I find it hard to understand her total faith. I don't believe I ever saw, even once, when she lost her belief that Jesus would cure her.

Once home we settled back into our organic diet and juicing and everything else we were doing to build up her immune system, as we had been doing for many months.

GOD'S PHONE CALL

One morning a short time later Maxine was home alone and the phone rang. It turned out to be a wrong number; however the man did identify himself. Before Maxine hung up she blurted out, "Are you Bill, who went to The Chapel years ago?"

He said, "Yes, why?"

She identified herself and sure enough they had known each other for almost 30 years through a previous church and had not seen each other in about 15. Maxine found out from Bill that a church nearby had started a healing room such as the one in the Spokane area. Her faith was kindled like I could not believe and she was off and running. She got the address of the church and made plans for her, Janet and Susan to go the next Tuesday evening.

Can you imagine a wrong number turning out that way? Bill was actually calling a number that was supposed to be a friend's house where his wife was that day, and misdialed by one or two numbers and got our house. Maxine, of course, told me that it was divine intervention, and I had to agree that maybe it was.

By this time I had read the Bible for the second time in my life, and was starting to understand what true faith was. I also liked the people I was meeting since it was the first time in my life I was getting to know people who kept their word, walked the talk, and truly lived by the Bible. To me this was very refreshing and I loved it. I was beginning to mimic Maxine in total belief that God would heal her and that we would have a long, happy life together. I believed that there was no way God would let her die since he had gone to such great lengths to bring us together.

Even if I didn't believe in faith healing, the Bible and Jesus were moving deeper and deeper into my heart and I relied on the Word in the Bible more and more for comfort. The more I read and understood, the more I knew that if I did lose her that she would be far better off than myself. She would be in the fullness of joy, while I would be the one that was hurting.

However, at this time I didn't know just how much pain that loss would be to me. Today I wish every day that I didn't have to know.

NEWCASTLE

That Tuesday, Maxine, Janet and Susan left the house and drove to The Healing Rooms in a church in the town of Newcastle. I stayed home. I felt she needed some time with her friends to talk and just do whatever women do when they are off and running. When they got home she was all excited and insisting that I go with her the next week. Well, I did promise her that I would go to whatever treatment she felt she needed, so I agreed

The next Tuesday evening I took her over to The Healing Rooms where we met Janet and Susan. I was able to experience firsthand what Maxine was so excited about the week before. Within five minutes of entering the room, I could feel something in the air. This was not like me; so at first I was very uneasy about the place, but that did not last long. Again, I got the feeling that maybe there was something to this "faith healing" because I wanted to believe and see it happen. The pastor talked for about a half hour before the teams began to pray for people. The teams doing the praying were touching each person needing prayer and they were deeply involved in praying for them. Some people needing prayer had to lie down and there were blankets available to keep them warm. Everyone was very pleasant and they truly believed that they could create an atmosphere of Divine Healing within that room. I was beginning to believe that it just might be possible.

For the next couple days after we left The Healing Rooms that Tuesday, Maxine seemed to have a burst of strength and to feel a lot like her old self. Because of the joy that it brought her I agreed to take her over to Newcastle each week for prayer. I also saw that she would have several days of no pain in her arm and chest after being prayed for at The Healing Rooms. But the infected lymph node on the right side of her chest and the breast tumors continued growing and causing a great deal of pain. We could now physically see the lump on her upper chest, and it was starting to protrude. We had been told that the doctors could not reach it with surgery and I'm not sure Maxine would have done it even if they could have. She was tired of being cut on.

The Healing Rooms gave us some hope and we continued to go there each week for many months, up to the point where Maxine would have to lie down the minute we got there and let them pray for her in that position.

As we moved into the middle of 2002 the lymph node that was infected on her chest was now showing as a lump the size of a large marble. She was getting weaker and weaker and would soon be in a wheelchair. I watched this progression go on and on with nothing I could do and I was dying inside. I was her crutch when we walked anywhere and she even had to get a disabled parking pass by that time so that I could park close to the places she wanted to go. By August of 2002 she could only walk about 20 or 30 feet before having to rest.

THINGS TO REMEMBER:

- ◆ The Bible and Jesus are there for you anytime you want to pick up and read and get to know them. I hope you do, because it will be a great comfort to you throughout your trial.
- ◆ Never say no to her if she is excited about a treatment and wants you to go along. Even if it's one you are not sure you believe in. She wants you there because you are her number one supporter; at least you had better be.

CHAPTER 14

Optimum Health Institute (OHI)
April/May 2002

❖ ❖ ❖

It is now springtime! But I do not see much evidence.
I'm taking it by faith.
— Maxine

In late April, 2002, Maxine and I and could barely handle rent payments along with all of the cancer treatments, and we were just getting by. I had not been able to find work for six months after the 9/11 disasters.

Mary Katherine Koppang, a close friend of Maxine's who was also battling breast cancer, told her about a clinic near San Diego, Optimum Health Institute (OHI). Mary Katherine told Maxine of the incredible difference going to this clinic had made for her. OHI is a natural health resort that has a program of eating only raw, live food and no meat or cooked food of any kind. They follow a diet that was created in the early 1900's by a woman named Ann Wigmore. They also teach people how to prepare live food and what foods not to mix with others.

Maxine had looked into natural health clinics around the country and even in Mexico and found that the usual cost for one person was around six thousand dollars per week. OHI (San Diego, CA and Austin, TX) is a ministry run by the Free Sacred Trinity Church and relies on volunteers. Because of this they are able to charge from six hundred to nine hundred dollars a week.

Still, there was no way we could afford it. We were already losing our property in Eastern Washington and had depleted both of our retirement funds along with having sold everything we could think of to keep her treatments and organic food going. We had been reduced to getting food stamps by this time and were months behind on our rent, not to mention maxed out on all our credit cards. Our phone never stopped ringing from creditors wanting money that I could not give them. Everything we had went to her cancer battle and I was glad to give it.

REJECTING THE URGE TO RUN

As a professional engineer and a business owner, I don't know if anyone can imagine how I felt about this situation. At times I wanted to get into my car and drive and not stop. I could not, as a man, let myself even think about running away, however sometimes those thoughts crossed my mind and I had to fight to reject them. Doctors had told me that many men bail out and leave when the pressure of the cancer gets bad. We, ourselves, met so many women whose husbands ran out on them or would not support them and it was heartbreaking. If I had done that I would have hated myself for the rest of my life. I loved that woman more than life itself. I even prayed to God that he would take the cancer from her and give it to me if someone had to have it. I would have done anything to be able to protect her.

I had sworn to her that I would be there no matter how hard it got because no matter how hard it was for me, I had to think about what she was going through. I would stay by her and be her support that she could always count on.

I was getting very scared because the lymph node in her chest was visibly growing and now she was unable to lift her right arm due to the pain. I had to get something done but had no I idea what to do to come up with the money. All we could do was pray for it and hope God would answer our prayers.

ANSWERED PRAYER

He did in the most wonderful way I could imagine. The Koppangs belonged to a little church of only about 30 people and they decided to adopt Maxine. They came up with enough money to send her to OHI for a week, along with the price of a round-trip airline ticket. At the same time, our church small group that met each Sunday after service took up a collection and gave us enough money for her to stay a second week. We were so thankful for these people and their generosity that we could not express it in words.

DINNER INVITATION

A few weeks prior to Maxine's departure, Mary Katherine and her husband John invited us to come have dinner and share more information about OHI. I had never met these folks prior to that day, but I liked them immediately when I did. We all sat down and talked for about an hour before dinner and it was a very enjoyable time for me.

When Mary Katherine said dinner was ready and on the table, I was ready for it. We sat down and I was given this wonderful salad with no dressing. I looked around.

Maxine smiled a funny smile. "There's no dressing, hon."

Okay, I could deal with that. I found some salt and used that. It was a very good salad and I was ready for the main part of the meal when Maxine said, "Mary Katherine, that was just wonderful."

"Really good," said John. He pushed back his chair and started clearing the dishes.

I looked at Maxine and she kicked me so hard in the leg I knew I had a bruise. It meant for me to shut up, so I did, still wondering where dinner was.

Everyone went out on the deck to talk. I was at a loss. What was going on? I tried to sit there and smile and be nice. After another hour or so Maxine got up. "I'm getting really tired. We should probably go."

We got into the car and had just started down the road when I was not going to keep quiet any longer. Before I could say a word, she leaned over to kiss me on the cheek. "You were so considerate, honey. Thank you! You can stop at the first place we find and get something to eat."

Unbeknownst to me, Maxine and Mary Katherine had decided to have a dinner that would be completely like what would be served at OHI. That meant all raw vegetables, no cooked food and no meat. Everyone that was to be at this dinner knew about this OHI meal except me. Maxine was rather sure that I would not have come or would have insisted on stopping so I could get a burger or something if I knew.

By the way, the Koppangs invited me over for a "real" normal dinner after I lost Maxine and they do serve a great meal.

BEING APART

Once Maxine arrived at OHI, friends, family and church members were asking me if they could do anything for her. I told them that she loved to get cards in the mail. I wanted her to know I was thinking of her, too, so I sent a card to her each day she was down there alone.

The truth was that I was having a really bad time of being alone. It was pure hell not being able to see her and take care of her, and I was unable to sleep at all. I am a disabled veteran so I finally decided to go up to the VA hospital in Seattle and see if they could help me with my sleep. When I told the nurse at the desk my situation and that I needed something for sleep, she figured I needed mental help. Maybe she was right; I don't know. She set me up to see one of the mental health doctors and we talked for about an hour. He decided that I did need some kind of sleeping medication and provided me with enough to last until Maxine got home. He also wanted me to take some sort of stress-reducing pill. I never was sure what that was, nor was I going to take any of it. The sleeping pills did help me sleep, and because I was getting some rest I was able to start thinking a lot more clearly. I must admit that I was an emotional mess by this time. We had been fighting breast cancer for over two years and Maxine was not getting better. More cancer just kept showing up. I hurt in my heart and there was nothing I could do to get relief from that hurt.

OHI

When Maxine called the first Thursday she was so weak she could barely stand up. She explained that it was natural for a person to react this way because she was on a very powerful detox and the body was working hard to eliminate all toxins within it. Still, it was hard not to worry.

At the end of the first week Maxine was on the phone again. "I feel great!" she said. Her voice sounded like the old Maxine

— always bubbly and happy. I had not heard her talk like that in two years and, to say the least, I was thrilled to hear it.

She told me about meeting a guy named Fred Travalena. For those of you who are too young to know, Fred was the world's greatest impersonator in the 60s and 70s. He was on most of the television shows such as The Tonight Show. She found out that he was a born-again Christian and they, along with a group of about eight people, would get together each evening after dinner and pray.

She also told me about meeting the woman who played the original Cat Woman on the old Batman series. She was now a naturopath, and Maxine could call her for help anytime she felt the need. It was clear to me that Maxine was doing well on that diet, even though when she explained what she was eating, it sounded really bad. She told me that they didn't serve anything that had been cooked. It was a pure vegetable diet prepared in many different ways. They had lettuce, sprouts, beans, broccoli, asparagus, etc. All raw, with no normal seasoning.

Maxine wanted to stay down there for another two weeks since the plan they had took four weeks to complete, but we could not afford it. Well, here came the Koppangs and our community group again. The money for her extra stay came in within two days and when I called to tell her, she was so excited she told me that she wanted me down there because she did not like being away from me for so long. I told her I would do what I could, but not to get her hopes up.

The next day my youngest son called and said, "Dad, you need to be down there with her, so I'm buying your plane ticket on my bank card and you can pay me back when you can." I was stunned. This kid was putting himself through the university with no help from me or anyone else and he wanted to send me to California to be with his stepmom. The ticket was now covered and my share of the stay would come in the next day from (again) the Koppangs' small church. Not only did they give me the money to be down there, but when they found out my 20-year-old son put the price of the plane ticket on his credit card, they came up with the money to pay him back. They told me that he had enough to deal with and that they could afford it better than him. In a situation like this I don't care how big or tough a guy may think he is, I guarantee he will be in tears. I sure was. I was unable to even talk I was so grateful to everyone. I was on my way two days later.

CHANGES

I got to San Diego on a Saturday afternoon and caught a cab to Lemon Grove. The drive only took about a half an hour and it was hot and clear and beautiful out. The taxi driver found OHI and drove in the gate to drop me in the back where Maxine had told me to go. I found her room on the second floor and knocked on the door. I hardly recognized the woman who greeted me with *both* arms outstretched. She landed on me, almost knocking me over. She was beaming with a huge smile and bouncing like a school kid. I was overwhelmed by her energy since she had not had much since 1999. She stepped back and showed me that she was able to do full circles with her right arm and lift whatever she wanted to with no pain. She said that the diet, exercise, and meditation had been working beyond what she had hoped for. Seeing what she was now able to do made me believe it also.

She had put up a big ribbon across the room with a sign that read "Welcome My Love." We stood there holding each other for about 10 minutes. Then she stepped back and said, "Guess what we are doing tomorrow?"

Of course, I had no idea; I thought we were going to eat sprouts and sit around in classes all day. Not this Sunday apparently. She had made plans for us to go with several other women to Tijuana, Mexico for the day. I was not as thrilled at this as she was since I had been there in 1971 and 1972 when I was in the Marine Corps and it was not a place I would want to take a woman like Maxine. She insisted, so we planned on the trip.

TIJUANA

The next morning we were up and packed in with three other women on our way to Mexico. It was the second week of May and it was very hot outside the air-conditioned car. I sat there wondering how this was all going to turn out. I knew that Maxine could not tolerate the heat very well and I also knew that she did not like dirty and foul places where safety was questionable. That was the way it was in Tijuana in the early '70s when I had been there.

We parked on the US side and started walking towards the border. I should have known that everything would be considerably different from when I was last there. Back in '71, I'd walked through the guard gate onto a dusty old trail and over a decrepit bridge to get into town, where there was nothing but filth and bars. Now it was all cleaned up with nicely paved walkways and roads. Maxine was quick to let me know how wrong I had been to worry about anything. It sure irritated me that she ended up being right so often.

Anyway, we got to the town and what a difference 30 years had made. The streets were clean, the shops were in mini-malls and there were no drunks anywhere that I saw. Now that I had relaxed somewhat, she started shopping. This was something Maxine was able to do very well. One of the women with us spoke Spanish and had even lived in Tijuana for several years and that was a big help when it came to bargaining over a price.

I never saw anything like it: the shopkeeper, our Spanish-speaking friend and Maxine all standing in a circle waving their arms and talking at the same time. I'm not sure how it was accomplished but she managed to purchase several items for very little. I was proud of the way she could get things for a fraction of the price on the tags.

We spent most of the day in Tijuana and I even agreed to have lunch there, which I would have never done 30 years ago.

By late afternoon Maxine was almost ready to drop. She had pushed herself too much that day and had managed to dehydrate herself. We headed back and found out that we would be standing in line for almost two hours to get back over the border. She was really feeling badly by now and I was upset with myself for not insisting we return earlier.

We finally got across the border, but we had gotten separated from the other three and they were not at the car yet. I had to get her out of the sun so we walked up to a restaurant and had some dinner and a lot of water. Maxine could have run all day and night prior to the cancer, but now I almost had to carry her back to the car. She was in physical pain and I was in emotional pain. It hurts so much to see your wife lose her strength and almost collapse in your arms when only a few years earlier she could almost out-go you. Thank God the others were back at the car when we came from the restaurant. Maxine needed to get to her bed and rest.

THE PLAN

We finally made it back to OHI and we were so tired we just went to bed since we had to be up at exercise class at 7am. This would be my first day of the plan and I was both excited and nervous about it. I had been wondering what I had gotten myself into in my desire to always be with her.

Morning came and she was ready to go again. It was refreshing to see her like that; it had been a long time since she was able to bounce back that fast. This was my first official day at OHI and I had no idea what I was in for. Exercise class was easy for me since I have always stayed in shape. I loved watching Maxine do the exercises she'd been unable to do before at home. Then came breakfast — or I guess you could call it breakfast. It was sprouts and grass and piles of seeds and some sort of dip or sauce made of who knows what. She loved it and was eating every bite. I picked at it and looked for some salt but, alas, there was none to be found.

By lunch I was tired of classes. They were very interesting, but I was very hungry. Once again, we were given another plate of the same type of food as breakfast, only more and different-looking stuff. I was trying very hard to eat what they gave us and Maxine was very nicely trying to get me to do so, but I just could not get it down. She would eat two plates full and pick at mine, while I was lucky to get half of one plateful down. Being the sweetheart she was, she would never push me too hard and would only remind me, "If a 130-pound woman can eat two platefuls, honey, then a 200-pound man needs more than half of one to stay healthy."

The same thing happened at dinner and I went to bed very hungry that night.

On Tuesday it got even worse when my only food was a glass of juice for breakfast, lunch and dinner. It was the same Wednesday and by that afternoon I had lost 13 pounds and was getting so weak I could hardly get around. I told Maxine that I loved her and I knew how much this place and this diet had helped her, but I was starving. She let me go downtown (without telling anyone) and have a whopper or two at Burger King along with about a pound of fries. Within minutes I could feel my strength coming back. I had promised her that I would take any and all treatments she had so that she would not have to be alone, but even she agreed that every third day I could to go downtown and get some meat. I did however like the amount of weight I had lost.

One of our daily requirements was to juice and drink four to six ounces of pure wheat grass juice. OHI had a room where they grew the wheat grass all year long and another room where they had about eight juicing machines. The first time I tasted the juice I found it to be almost intolerable. All of the classes told us that it was very good for us and that we needed to drink it so I forced myself to do so. After a few days I did get used to it and was able to go along with their program. Maxine had several books at home about the benefits of wheat grass juice and she had been drinking it for about a year. This, however, was the first time for me. I did make it through that week and I will say that I was not as sorry about the idea of going home as Maxine was.

Believe it or not I was able to get used to the food and felt great by Saturday, just as they said I would. I wished that I could move down there and keep her at OHI for about nine months. In my heart I believe she would have beaten the cancer had I been able to afford that.

A Gift

We got ready to leave that Saturday morning and were sitting in the lunchroom waiting for our ride when the director of OHI in both Lemon Grove and Austin walked over and asked to speak with Maxine. A few minutes later Maxine came running back and grabbed me and said we had been given a free week and also a beautiful new room. I asked why and she said that the director told her that the employees of OHI liked us and voted to have us stay another week so Maxine could have the benefit of the entire four-week course. They had a scholarship program, allowing employees to choose. This was such a special thing for them to do for us, but I can guarantee it was because of Maxine, not me. She had made friends with everyone staying or working there in that first three weeks. I spent over an hour on the phone making new plans, taking care of things at home, getting help with the mail and paper, etc. I was so happy for her. However I knew I was in for another week of uncooked, no-meat meals.

This also gave me a chance to repay Terry and Susan Newby for all that they had done for us over the months. I had made arrangements for Maxine and me to have a four-day anniversary at Ocean Shores the next weekend in our Trend West condo (the only thing we had managed to save). Since we were going to stay another week we were not going to be able to use the time. I called and transferred it into Terry's name and told them to go have a weekend on us. That weekend was going to be our anniversary weekend, but it worked out to be the Newby's anniversary weekend and we were extremely happy to be able to give it to them.

The second week was a lot better for me and I even got to the point where I could eat almost all of the raw food. I guess if you are hungry enough you get to like anything. Besides the food, the grounds at OHI were beautiful. There is a park-like front area where everyone sits around in lawn chairs and relaxes in the sun after or during a meal. The pool was a ways off from the main building but was really nice on the days when it was 100 degrees or hotter.

For some reason hummingbirds were everywhere and we found several nests on the grounds. These birds did not seem to mind us being there and had their nests so low we could walk by and look into them and watch them raising their babies. If you thought hummingbirds were small, you should see baby hummingbirds. They are less than the size of a fingernail. At our home in Kent, Maxine always had four or five hummingbird feeders hanging from March until August. They were her favorite bird and she made sure they knew they were very welcome.

Being able to watch these little birds was a joy to her and seeing the babies in a nest was almost unbelievable. Even with the cancer that was eating at her she was truly happy. I loved it when she would lean on me for support so that she could stay just a little longer and watch.

Although I was getting used to the food, I still had to go to town every third day and get something more. One day I picked up a bottle of salad dressing and snuck it back to my room. Then each meal I would go to our room and load up on the dressing and then go out and sit with Maxine and the others to eat. Several people commented on how well I was doing. Maxine was sweet enough to laugh and agree with them, knowing full well that I was cheating.

We got through my week two and her week four and finally had to leave and fly home. I was happy to be going home but sad because of the incredible difference OHI had made in her health. We had learned so much about staying healthy from the classes that I recommend a week there to my friends, sick or well.

Maxine was working with the staff at OHI to see if she could be a missionary, which meant she could live next door in some apartments, work eighteen hours a week at OHI and stay on their complete program as long as she wanted. I wanted that for her so much that we talked about it all the way home and long into that first night back. By morning reality set in with me and I knew that there was no money for that to happen. It would take six hundred dollars a month and we did not have the extra money to make it happen. I was still out of work and it had been over six months now with no work in sight.

WORK

As it turned out, I wouldn't be back to work until June when I decided to give up on engineering and went to the Labor Union in Seattle to look for work. I had put myself through college when I was young working as a laborer on heavy construction so I figured I could maybe do it again. I did get lucky and on the work board was a request for a grade checker. Being a licensed civil engineer I sure knew how to check grade. I got the job and started working. The grade checking was okay and I did rather well, however on some days I had to do labor work and I tell you that I was not in the shape to do what I did 30 years before. But it was work, and I needed to do whatever I could to keep money coming in. This was the beginning of when our church became so special to us that I cannot express the gratitude we had towards them. I'm still grateful.

THINGS TO REMEMBER:

- ◆ You may be feeling guilty due to lack of money, but it's a trap that we cannot allow ourselves to fall into. We are only able to do so much, and we should not allow ourselves to feel guilty. I'm fighting this one as much as you may be.
- ◆ I advise you to be there for her and let her hang on and stop whenever she needs to rest. Never, ever make her rush or feel like you are irritated with her because she is slowing you down.

◆ Don't ever leave her for any reason. Be there no matter how hard it gets, because no matter how hard it is for you, just think about what she is going through. If you love her, then stay by her and be her support that she can always count on. Never allow your support to come into question.

CHAPTER 15

Radiation and Chemotherapy

❖ ❖ ❖

Faith doesn't come easy when you're wracked with pain.
The mornings — when energy is high and
the sun shines bright — are one thing.
But it's quite another in the midnight hours!
— Maxine

We got back from OHI in late May of 2002 and Maxine seemed to be doing well for a while. We tried to keep her on the OHI diet and exercise program as much as we could. It's a difficult program to follow at home but we were able to do about seventy percent of it. We bought only organic food and she ate only live, uncooked meals just as we did at OHI. Each morning she would set up her stereo outside the back sliding door and a soothing recorded voice would take her through her hour of exercises in the sunshine. She even had me tape her once so that she could show her friends what she did each morning.

Send in the Clowns

The fun part arose when our youngest son Bryan, 21 by that time, came home, looked out the window and saw what we were doing. He promptly came out and wanted in on the action. Maxine of course waved at him to join her.

Toes in, said the soothing voice. *Let your arms hang naturally. Chest up, shoulders back, lifting the torso out from the waist.*

"Are they serious?" Bryan started walking pigeon-toed behind Maxine.

Now turn your feet out the other direction, walking like a duck.

Bryan began a perfect Charlie Chaplin imitation, swinging an imaginary cane.

Tap your chest, aiding the immune system. It only takes a few taps.

Bryan beat his chest like a gorilla. Maxine was cracking up. That was the end of the film on special exercises.

Of course, we had to film an interview. "Bryan," said Maxine, "Since this is your first time doing the OHI Lymphatic Exercises, can you tell us how that has helped in your overall well-being?"

"Well all I basically need to say is," he removed his shirt, displaying a pretty impressive six-pack, "just look at me. This one exercise in ten minutes pumped me up!"

Maxine was bent over laughing.

"Yes, Maxine." Bryan struck an Adonis pose. "One morning."

"See?" said Maxine to the camera. "You can have this too. In just ten minutes a day!"

"And take your vitamins," Bryan added.

I still have that film and have shown it to a number of people that have found it absolutely hilarious. This was near the end of May of that year. We were running out of time and really did not know it yet.

Something is Wrong

In June or July of 2002 I started to notice some changes in Maxine. I could feel and sense something more was wrong than just the tumor on her chest but I could not put my finger on it. She just didn't seem right in her speech and the way she was doing things. I knew this woman very well and she simply was not being herself; however it was only in very minor ways. The way she would do things around the house and/or forget things made me wonder what else was going on. I could not pinpoint anything so I was unable to describe what I was sensing to the doctors or anyone else. I was getting very nervous and jumpy about the whole thing and yet I had no proof of anything to justify my feelings. It was like something was trying to tell me something but I was not smart enough to understand what it was. It was very frustrating for me and I kept asking God to help me understand what it was I was feeling.

Aolani: A Godsend

At that time we were fortunate that I was working and that Aolani had returned after graduating from college and working as an intern for a company in Oregon. Maxine's mother had recently moved to Dallas, Texas to live with her sister and Aolani was now renting her grandmother's home in Renton. Aolani was a real Godsend for me because she took over a lot of the care and appointments so that I could work more. Maxine was very happy too since she really liked having her daughter around and close to her. We split up the doctor appointments so that each of us could work and still one of us would be with Maxine. She always wanted one of us with her.

By the end of July I had picked up another job working for a local city as a project engineer and that made it a lot easier on me physically and financially.

A BAD FEELING

Sometime in August Maxine started talking to me about wanting to fly down to Dallas to visit her sister, Eleana, and her mother for a week or so. A year earlier she had flown down for a week of vacation paid for by Eleana. At the time I had asked if this could happen again sometime. But now I was very much against her going. "Don't even think about it," I told her.

We even got into arguments about it, which was wrong on my part but for some reason everything in me told me not to let her go. This went on for a month or two. She kept pestering me to let her go, but I held my ground and said, "No."

This was creating a bad situation within our house because she really wanted to go and I absolutely did not want her to. I knew that if she went something very bad would happen. I have no explanation for this feeling but I was not going to let it pass. Maxine even got nervous about it because she had seen me get these feelings before and they had saved us from being in a bad situation several times. Finally she decided to call my older sister, Wilma. "I'm going to tell your sister on you," she said. "I'm going to tell her how bad you're being for not letting me go."

Well, that didn't turn out as she had hoped.

"Is there some physical reason Alan's not willing to let you go?" Wilma asked her.

"I don't know," Maxine admitted.

The two of them decided that maybe Maxine had better go to a doctor and have a check-up before talking to me again.

TESTING

By then it was early September. On September 13th, Aolani took Maxine to a highly recommended doctor and had tests done to see if anything else was happening. When I got home from work Maxine was standing in the front room waiting for me. Her face told the story.

I pulled her to me, not saying anything. She threw her arms around my neck and almost crushed me hanging on. She was crying and talking at the same time. I couldn't understand what she was saying, but I started crying too.

After we both calmed down enough so she could talk and I could hear her, she told me that the tests revealed multiple spots of cancer in her brain. Without steroids to reduce the inflammation, getting on that airplane could have caused dangerous swelling of the tumors due to the pressure difference. She could have died on the airplane. Her doctor told her that there was no way she should consider flying anywhere. She must have thanked me a hundred times over the next week for sticking with my gut feeling and saying no to her, even when saying no hurt me so bad. I'd hated doing that, but was so glad I did.

We now had no choices left but radiation to the head to kill the cancer in Maxine's brain. If she did not have this treatment, doctors were anticipating she would not last more than a month or so. All the small changes that I had been sensing and seeing were a result of the cancer causing pressure on her brain.

THE BEST PART OF HER

Maxine started taking radiation treatments the next week and of course that meant she was going to lose her beautiful blonde hair. This was really traumatic for Maxine since she had always believed that her hair was her best feature.

Her sister and daughter took her to her favorite stylist and she had her hair cut into a short pixie cut and made something of a party of it. That seemed to work out okay until she was home alone with me that night. I found her looking at herself in the mirror and crying. I walked up behind her and put my arms around her.

"I'm losing the best part of myself," she said.

I laughed and made her turn around to face me. "You're wrong, Max. You're so wrong. It's not your hair that makes you special. It's your sweet, beautiful smile. It's the way you love everyone you've ever met. Those are the best parts of you. That's why so many people love you. I've been watching you for almost five years, baby. Every time you meet someone new, they can tell within a couple of minutes that you're really interested in them. You love them openly for who they are."

She looked at me, surprised. Maxine had the ability to spread love more than anyone I had ever known or seen, and she didn't even realize it.

MOVING

Due to the radiation Maxine was now not able to get around walking much so she was in a wheelchair most of the time. She seemed to take it in stride, while I was torn apart watching her get weaker and weaker. We had gotten the wheelchair for her in September to help her get around when we went places. By the time she was two weeks into the radiation she needed it all the time. This meant that the house we were renting would no longer work for us. It had three sets of steps and she was unable to get up and down them. She wanted a house that was one floor and while I was at work she spent time looking for one. After awhile she found exactly what she wanted and made arrangements to rent it.

The problem was that it would be a considerable task trying to get moved and she was not able to help at all. So Maxine moved into her daughter's house for a short time so that I could get us moved and the new house ready for us. I would work during the day, move stuff in the afternoon, and then most nights I would go to her daughter's house and sleep on a pad next to Maxine's bed.

It was now November of 2002, and everything started out just fine the first week with me moving a trailer and truckload each night after work. On the first weekend I even got help from a number of the men from our church. The second week I was doing okay and it looked like I was right on schedule even with the problems Maxine was having, but things never seem to work the way you plan.

COMPLICATIONS

During the second week Maxine developed pneumonia and was taken to the hospital in an ambulance and put on IV medications. Now I was running up to the hospital in Seattle to stay every other night and was not able to do any moving on those nights.

The really unexpected problem started just after I delivered an unneeded computer table to the home of our administrative pastor, who was helping us move. I had just left the pastor's house and driven to the next intersection. I was sitting at the light waiting to turn left. I had decided to treat myself to a mocha before heading home and then to the hospital. As I was waiting I was suddenly blasted forward. A woman in a minivan had slammed into the back of my small utility trailer at over thirty-five miles an hour. I was pushed ahead into the intersection about fifteen feet.

I sat there for a few seconds, somewhat stunned, before I could get out and see what had happened. I walked back and asked if she was okay and noticed she had at least two small children in the back of the van. I asked if they were all right and she said yes. I'm not sure what I would have done if she had said no because I was almost ready to fall down myself. I got back to my truck and pulled it into a parking lot by a small store. The bumper was dragging on the ground and my trailer was a mess, along with the entire back of my truck.

I walked into the store after calling the police and I ordered my mocha. I was really feeling strange, so I went back and sat down in my truck until the police arrived. The officer wrote up a report and ticketed the woman and told me to try and take my truck and trailer home. I asked him to check the lights on my trailer and he did. Only one was not working and I lived close by. The officer and I were both a little concerned about the bumper dragging and the trailer barely hanging on. He followed me most the way home and I did make it. That is, to the old house that was nearby but had no furniture anymore.

I went in and sat on the floor for awhile to try to get my head straight. After about 15 minutes I decided I had better try to get to the Multi Care Center and get checked. My truck was not going to make it, so I was going to have to use my old Cadillac that only sometimes ran. It did get me there, but, of all the luck, the place was closed and the car barely got me back to the old house. I lay down on the floor this time and wondered if I should try to get to the hospital. As I was lying there, the ceiling started to spin and when I woke up it was morning.

I had passed out on the floor and woke up feeling badly. I had a headache and my back and neck were very painful along with a numbness running down my left leg. I had to lie there for awhile thinking of what I could do. Any movement at all hurt, but I had to get things done so I forced myself to get up. I called for a rental truck and they brought one out to the house for me. Fortunately I had rented trucks from Enterprise enough that they knew where I lived.

I made it to the clinic and the doctor told me all I had to do was take some pain pills, muscle relaxants and an anti-inflammatory. That would have been good if I'd wanted to cover up my problem, but I felt something was wrong and covering it up was not going to help. I tried to get by on the pain pills for the rest of the day before I called my chiropractor and set up an appointment with him for later that day.

It took me a while to get to his office, and I was not feeling very well when I arrived. He took x-rays and found that my neck was badly out of place and three disks were out in my lower back. He very gently worked on my neck and back and set me up for a weekly appointment and massage therapy as well. When I left an hour later, I felt better but not good. Driving back to the house I realized that I had not seen or contacted Maxine in over 48 hours. I wasn't even sure how long at that point.

I called Maxine's hospital room and she answered. I could tell she was really upset as I explained what had happened to me. I headed to the hospital to see her and of course I did not know it yet, but she'd had a bad situation happening to her at the same time. She had been retaining fluid, as often happens to bedridden patients, and her legs had swollen painfully to about twice their normal size. She had been worried about me and had been calling all of our friends to ask if they had seen me. Of course they hadn't, since they did not know what had happened or where I was.

My back, neck and head were hurting so badly that I was unable to stay with her that night and had to go home to the new house and figure out where I could sleep. I ended up on a pile of bedding on one of my son's beds. I didn't have anything ready and now I was unable to lift anything, so I could not complete our moving. Fortunately, Maxine's swelling came down and she was well enough to be released a few days later. She went back to Aolani's house. I, on the other hand, had to figure out what I could do with our house but was in no shape to do it.

PUSHED TO THE LIMIT

For the next three to four weeks I would try to go to work, but was having a hard time since the neck problem was giving me severe headaches and I would have to go home. At first my plan was to continue sleeping on a pad next to Maxine's bed at her daughter's, but that lasted only one night. By morning I was almost unable to move my back, neck or legs and the headache was unreal. Maxine and I had to be happy with seeing each other in the evening and on weekends since I could not stay there and I was unable to lift to be able to fix up our new house. Our plan of a couple of weeks apart to move turned into almost three months, due to that accident. To me that was almost hell on earth. I felt I had been cheated out of time in my life with her. Knowing how weak she was had me going to bed every night during that time scared to death that I wouldn't see her again.

TOGETHER AGAIN

I finally managed to get feeling a little better and got the house fixed up enough so that she could move back in. She had a hospital bed by now and we put it in the spare room so she could have a room of her own. This was okay for a short time, but we both decided we did not like to sleep away from each other. I took our queen bed and put it in the spare room and put her hospital bed in our room. I then loaded her into her wheelchair and we got into the truck and went out shopping for a single bed.

We found one she liked and took it home and placed it next to the hospital bed for me so we could sleep together again. I had missed that very much and judging from her reaction so had she. The radiation to her head had been hard on her. It caused her to have difficulty speaking and remembering what she was talking about. She seemed weak and for the first few weeks she was not able to even walk around the house. Gradually, she seemed to come out of it and was talking more clearly and moving a lot better day by day. We were just a little hopeful.

CHEMOTHERAPY

Sometime during the later stages of the radiation, Maxine made a decision to discuss the idea of taking chemotherapy along with radiation to her breast and the lymph node in her chest. I'm not sure what exactly made her do this and it's best if I never find out. If I ever found out that someone had talked her into it I would not accept responsibility for what I might say or do to that person. I am going to believe that it was her choice based on her feeling that all other alternatives had been exhausted.

While she was having the radiation treatments to her head she was also taking morphine for the pain. She was not thinking properly during this time and would agree to things that she never would have if she understood or was in her right mind. As it was, she was talked into a couple of things that she would have never done otherwise and as soon as her mind cleared after the radiation she and I made the necessary changes to see to it that it never happened again. We went to our attorney and had him draft new wills along with durable power of attorney both ways. Maxine wrote a list of everything she wanted done in case she was to lose her battle with the cancer. I believe we both knew then that time was running out and she wanted to get everything in order.

Maxine and I knew from the very start in 1999 that chemo would not have any effect on the cancer, but would destroy her immune system and allow the cancer free reign to grow within her system and kill her. This is why I was very surprised the day she told me she had talked to the oncologist at Swedish Hospital and was considering taking chemo. I asked her why, since she knew that no chemo would help, would she even consider it. She said her oncologist had told her of a new chemo that might work and that she would only have to take one dose a week for six weeks. If it was not helping they would stop.

Now during this time Maxine started having weekly radiation on her breast and lymph node tumor on her right side. Thank God she was done with the radiation to her brain. She was already weak from that and I was not at all agreeable to chemo. However, back when it all started I had promised her that if she made a decision, whether I agreed or not, I would back her one-hundred percent. I did inform her that I was against the chemo entirely, because there was no proof or even the slightest indication that they had found one that would work.

It was bad enough for me to see this once very active, beautiful woman be weakened as much as she was by the radiation; but now she was taking chemo and what I watched over the next few months devastated me. She ended up having only three treatments of the chemo because of how badly she was affected by it, but that was all it took. The poison the doctors put into her destroyed her immune system and the only thing that was growing and thriving was the cancer. As I suspected, the chemo could not do anything against the cancer and had only weakened her immune system. Maxine was now very rapidly losing what little strength she had.

THINGS TO REMEMBER:

- ◆ Don't let yourself be swayed if you get a very strong gut feeling about something that may be dangerous to her health. Go with the feeling. There's a good chance you may be right.

- ◆ Radiation causes many different side effects, so you will have to be ready for almost anything. She will need more help than ever before and you need to be the one giving it. You will be very glad you were there for her.

- ◆ As soon as you find cancer or any terminal disease in either of you make sure to complete your wills and both of you get durable power of attorney each way. Don't allow some social worker or other person to talk you or your wife into signing the rights over to anyone else.

CHAPTER 16

Her Faith in Jesus

◆ ◆ ◆

*I love walking the tree-lined driveway — my cathedral,
my haven of God-given beauty — alone. This is my
favorite place and time of day. It's the time I can talk
things over with the King of Kings, who also happens to
be my loving Heavenly Father. Sometimes I laugh as
I walk. Sometimes I cry. Mostly I pray in tongues — but
also in English (always out loud), and I quote scripture
to the Lord, the birds, the trees and myself. Sometimes
I actually practice future sermons. The Lord is doing
some deep, cleansing work in my life.*

— *Maxine*

Maxine had a faith in the Lord that was stronger than any
I have ever seen. She didn't have to tell anyone that she
was a Christian because she showed it in her actions. She lived
that which she spoke and believed. I think this was one of the
biggest attractions I found in this woman: a woman who

walked the walk and didn't even have to talk about it for others to know what she was. She loved almost everyone she met and everyone seemed to love her.

WELL-LOVED

I had never known anyone who had as many friends as she had. When Maxine and I took a day trip to Ocean Shores on our third date, we had so much fun down there we didn't get back to her condo until midnight. She had about eight phone messages from friends checking up on her, wondering if that "new guy" she was seeing had kidnapped her or something. Thankfully, she told me she would call each one after I left and assure them that she was all right and that I was okay.

When I read Maxine's diary after she died, I found that she quoted scripture or wrote a small prayer almost every day from the first day we found the tumor in 1999. She would praise God in her writing and in her speech during the day.

IN THE SPIRIT

Once a week, Maxine and a couple of her friends would get together for a prayer meeting. The first time the three of them were at our house my son Chris was home and I knew there were going to be some questions. You see, Maxine and her friends were tongue-talking Christians. Tongues, according to the Bible, is a prayer language given by the Holy Spirit for the perfect prayer. Chris had never seen or heard of such a thing. Once the praying got started Chris heard noise but could not understand what was being said. He came to the door of the front room and just stood looking at these three women making sounds that made no sense to him at all. He was about to say something when I spotted him and grabbed him and led him into another room. I explained what it was about and he stood there shaking his head and groaning. He came up with an excuse to leave the house and didn't come back until he called me to be sure that they were done.

TRUE FAITH

Maxine made a Christian out of me over a very short period of time, simply because of how she was. She introduced me to people who were true Christians — the kind of people I'd always wished I could meet. She believed that Jesus was always with her and that God would either heal her or take her home to be with Him. She really wanted to stay around and have a long life with her husband. She even got mad at God a few times — maybe more than I know. However, right up to her last day on this earth she was true to her faith.

She wanted so much to see the day when she and I would baptize my three sons at our church. She worked on the guys in her sweet way and was making very good progress with them, but she ran out of time. She made me promise that I would continue to work on them until they accepted Jesus and agreed to be baptized. "I want to be sure I'll see them again someday," she said. "And the only way I know how to do that is to see them in Heaven."

Each time she spoke of this it was like someone taking a knife and shoving it through my heart. I could not even let myself think of the idea of her not being there with us.

BAPTISM

The day I agreed to be baptized in front of everyone at our church, I believe had to be one of the best days of Maxine's life. I had never seen her so beautiful and alive. Maxine was the one that was going to baptize me and she was so thrilled that I would agree to it since she had been trying to get me to for some time. "I'm so happy," She hugged me. "You're going to have a new life, starting today."

Maxine and I had been told to wear shorts or a swimming suit for the baptism and so we each wore shorts. Mine were okay for a guy, but Maxine chose to wear very short black ones that looked really good on her size six rear end and tanned legs. We use a portable hot tub at our church. I was already standing in the tub with the pastor when Maxine lifted her leg up to get in, hiking the shorts up even more. From somewhere in the front row of the church came a long low whistle that only the first three or four rows heard. They all cracked up laughing. Most of the church could not figure out why those up front were laughing. Maxine had poor hearing, so she was confused but the pastor and I knew. I was laughing while he turned red, trying to ignore the entire event.

I bet I'm still the only person who has ever had his baptizer whistled at. When I told Maxine later what had happened she was embarrassed about it. I told her not to be. I was so proud that she looked so good she even got whistles in church.

GIVING THANKS IN ALL CIRCUMSTANCES

Maxine wrote in her journal that she believed Jesus would heal her and, if not, she that she would go to her reward loving and praising the Lord. In the end that is exactly what she did. Maxine praised the Lord up to the last minute of her life. She was truly a Biblical woman and wife and she never let her faith be challenged. She was afraid for a while that if she died of the cancer within her that I would hate the Lord for taking her so early. She had seen it happen with other men who had lost their wives to cancer. I assured her that would never be the case, for if I was to hate the Lord I would be condemning everything she ever believed in. That would be dishonoring to her, and that's not something I could ever do.

THINGS TO REMEMBER:

◆ Don't ever blame God for the death of a loved one, for that is dishonoring to the loved one and the only person that it will hurt is you. Also, if the loved one believed in God and you allow yourself to hate God, then that means you do not believe in your loved one. That would be tragic.

CHAPTER 17

Germany: A Lost Hope

◆ ◆ ◆

I am passionately desiring to see Jesus glorified in this
whole thing! I love Him and with His strength I will love
Him no matter what happens in my life.
— Maxine

Sometime around December of 2002 Maxine and I found
out about a treatment center in Germany called the St.
George Klinic that had been having great success in curing cancer using a system of heating the body up to 107 degrees and
holding it at that temperature until the cancer was destroyed.
As I understood it, the cancer cells could not live in over 105-
degree temperatures. This way only the cancer was killed and
the rest of the body was okay. It took about 24 hours to heat the
body up and then slowly cool it down to a normal temperature.
We contacted the clinic and asked if there was anyone we could
talk to in the Washington State area that had been there for
treatments. It turned out that a woman in Bellevue had just

returned from her second trip over there for treatment. We got her name and phone number and called her. She was very pleasant and invited us up to her home.

REASON FOR OPTIMISM?

By this time Maxine had lost her hair to the radiation. She was in a wheelchair most of the time and was very weak. The woman who met us was around 72, but looked about 10 years younger. She was full of life and was very happy to tell us about her trip to Germany and the treatment she received. She said she'd had cancer in a number of areas of her body and was completely out of hope for any cure or help at all in the United States. After hearing of this clinic from a friend, she and her husband had decided to pool all their money and send her over there with her daughter. She told us that she had been twice in the last two years and now had no sign of cancer. She said she'd started feeling better than she had in years after only the first treatment.

She also told us that if we got over there not to be surprised at the fact that an entire wing of the hospital is for Americans only. She said wealthy Americans go there to get treatment for cancer because the US does not allow these treatments within its borders. She told us that those with money would never waste their time being treated in the US. We had learned enough by then that we were not surprised at all by what she was saying. She gave us some literature and a videotape about the clinic and we were on our way home with new hope.

By the time we left the woman's home we were excited about this clinic, but still were a little skeptical and wanted more information. I was mentally jumping up and down with hope, and trying hard not to show it.

The Klinic e-mailed information about their facility along with costs for treatment, room and board. If we were to go there we could get a private room for the two of us for the cost of one. Anyone who comes from the US may bring one person with them for help and support. The cost of the stay along with the treatments was in the range of eight-thousand dollars per week. They recommended three weeks to get the full benefit of the treatments. Three weeks meant twenty-four thousand dollars and that did not include the airfare to get there and back. It was obvious to us that we would have to ask for help again if we were to even have a chance to do this. However, with the way the cancer was growing, we were looking at what may be Maxine's last hope.

AN UNEXPECTED ANSWER

We spent the rest of December trying to figure out how we were going to come up with more than twenty-four thousand dollars to pull off this trip. The last weekend of December we decided to take a trip over the mountains to visit my sister Wilma and brother-in-law Larry. It was to be a fun trip of relaxing at their house, sitting around talking, and taking it easy. We were on a mountain pass when a call came in on Maxine's cell phone. She was very surprised to hear the voice of Fred Travalena, whom she had met at OHI.

Fred had called Maxine to see how she was doing and how her battle was progressing. Maxine got somewhat shook up and started crying, so she handed the phone to me. I told Fred about the German clinic.

"Listen," said Fred, "If you can set it up, I'll come out there. I can put on a benefit show for her and we'll raise the money that way. Don't worry about my airfare, I can cover that."

I was so stunned I was almost unable to speak to him. I tried to control my emotions, drive, hold the phone and talk all at the same time. My heart was beating so fast I was almost sick and I needed to stop somewhere. Maxine was looking at me, wondering what was going on.

Our call ended with me telling Fred that I would get back to him as soon as possible. You see, he had prior engagements and only had the 10th of January open for the event. We had 10 to 12 days to get something ready for him or he would not be able to do it. Being an engineer, I had no idea how to do something like this, but I was very excited, even though somewhat shaken. This was the best news we had heard in a long time.

I pulled into the next rest stop and we sat there in the truck as I explained to Maxine everything Fred had said. We agreed that we should continue our trip, but we would return home that evening instead of staying the night so I could talk to people at New Community Church about Fred's offer and see if any of them had an idea of how to set up a benefit event. Our last trip to see relatives turned out to be a trip of renewed hopes

We ended up staying at Wilma and Larry's overnight anyway because Maxine was too weak to sit up in the truck for the two and-a-half hour drive home. The next morning we slept in a bit and then left very rested and full from one of Wilma's great breakfasts.

A MIRACLE OF COOPERATION

Once we arrived home I decided that I would go to the church office and talk to them about the possibility of the benefit show. I was not even sure it was possible to do in such a short time. I first talked to the office manager, Geri, explaining to her what had transpired the day before on the phone. She said that she would talk to her husband Mike and that he had some experience with this sort of thing.

Well, that's not all Geri had up her sleeve. When I left that office she must have called everyone in the church leadership, because things started happening so fast it was incredible. Mike called me later that day and asked if he could get Fred's phone number. I gave it to him and within two days they had produced posters, flyers, and signs along with a local newspaper story about Maxine. The show was to be held at the school where New Community met for Sunday services. Maxine and I ended up on the second page of the local newspaper with a beautiful story about her cancer battle and the drive to raise money for her trip to Germany.

Maxine and I were overwhelmed at the speed at which everything was coming together on her behalf. Never would I have thought that a show such as this could be planned in less than ten days and be successful. However, the word was getting out quickly. The cost of each ticket was only 10 dollars. Believe me; you would pay a lot more to see Fred perform anywhere else. I was hoping for a couple hundred people to show up. I didn't expect to raise more than two or three thousand dollars in such short notice. I thought that anything over that amount would be a bonus.

The night of the show came and was I surprised! The gym was packed. I'm not sure exactly how many people crammed into that gym, but I know that there were no empty chairs and no remaining room to put more chairs. They introduced Maxine, talked a little about her fight with cancer, and I wheeled her up to the front so that people could see her before Fred came on. Once Fred was introduced, he captured the audience completely. At over 60 years old this man did imper-sonations, comedy, sang, danced, and put on a show that got him three standing ovations. I don't believe anyone in the crowd expected the incredible show that he gave. When he was done, the crowd stood there giving him ovations that seem to keep going on and on.

I found out later that he gives several benefit shows a year to help cancer patients around the country. Along with being a great entertainer, Fred Travalena is a true Christian and humanitarian. I will never be able to thank him enough for what he did for us, for he too was fighting cancer.

The next Sunday at church Maxine was going to be given a check for the amount that was raised from the show. I was thinking that this would be a good step toward the money we needed to get to Germany and was thrilled about it. However, when the pastor announced that he had a check for $16,000 and another check for $5,000 more was coming, I almost fell out of my chair. Maxine was crying openly when handed the check and I was trying my best to stay composed. Never in our wildest dreams did we think that there would be that much money from that one night of laughter, but there it was. The trip to Germany was going to happen and we had a chance to beat the cancer. I had to take a trip to the barn again that night — not to beat on the walls in pain, but to cry out to God in thanks for all of the people who had helped put this impossible show together in such a short time. I still thank God for Mike and Geri Jefferies for taking the lead and making the entire thing happen.

By this time Maxine needed help daily and Aolani and I were stretched to the limit with our work and trading off with Maxine. At this time, the women of our church made up a schedule so that one of them was at our house every day to help Maxine while Aolani and I were at work. This was such a treat for

Maxine since she loved having people over. One day the music pastor and all of the singers came over and played music for her. She loved it. The music was the biggest reason she choose the church in the first place. Our music pastor wrote a lot of his own songs and I believe Maxine preferred them to any others.

Maxine and I were thrilled about the opportunity we now had. The money was in a new bank account so that we could account for each cent of it. I contacted St. George Klinic in Germany and sent them all the latest information on Maxine's cancer. We began making arrangements to travel there within a few weeks. All we were waiting for was the Klinic's treatment plan, and the date and time we were to arrive in Germany. We had not been so happy for a long time and we felt as though God had His hand in all of this.

HOPE DESTROYED

Our happiness came to a sudden halt with an e-mail that I received from St. George Klinic. It read, "Due to the weakened condition of Maxine, we do not believe we can be of any help for her." That's all it said. They didn't even bother to explain why. I e-mailed them and told them all we had done to get her there and how their treatments may be her last hope. I asked if they would reconsider.

The answer I got was just as short as the first message, "We don't believe she would survive the treatment."

This was almost more than I could take. I just sat at my

computer in tears, trying to figure out how to tell Maxine. This was just about our last hope of any help. The tumor on her chest was being radiated and was getting somewhat smaller, but the other cancer inside her body was running wild. I would have rather gone out and shot myself than have to tell her what they had said. I was so sick to my stomach and wrapped around the axle that I'm not sure how long I just sat there not moving.

I finally got up and walked into the room where Maxine was working on a craft project that she wanted to finish. I sat down next to her. Before I could even say a word she turned to me and said, "They won't let me come, will they?" I put my arms around her and she held me. "It's all right," she said.

I wanted to hold her tight enough to make the cancer leave her and come into my body. I felt so useless. She had known somehow that I would get that e-mail but she didn't want to tell me for fear of hurting me. She was dying of cancer and yet she wanted to protect me. How does a man find a woman who loves him that much? I wanted her to be well so badly I would have done anything to have it happen.

This time I had to go to the barn and the walls really took the pounding of their lives. I did this after she had gone to bed. I didn't want her to know what I was doing. She was already worried enough about me; she sure didn't need to worry any more. Losing a woman who loves you that much is so painful. You have no idea how hard it is to sit here and remember and write about it.

Apparently Maxine had felt at some point during all of the production that she just might be too sick to travel to Germany, or that they would not accept her in her weakened condition. I was far more broken up over the situation than she was. She took it in stride and told me that we would do what we could and that was all we could do.

OHI

We started talking about OHI again. She agreed that at OHI she had felt better than she had at any other time during the nearly three years we had been fighting cancer. We decided that we would use some of the event money to take another trip to OHI and see if she could regain her strength as she had done in March of 2002. If she could, we would then use the back VA disability check I would soon get to take her to Germany if they would accept her at a later date.

At least it was a possibility and I needed something to hang on to. I was a complete mess: I was having a hard time thinking straight and going to work was very difficult, even though everyone there was being sensitive about the situation and giving me a lot of breaks. We began to plan another trip to OHI.

CHAPTER 18

OHI 2003

◆ ◆ ◆

*God is using cancer to transform me. I have already
changed so much. Nothing is really the same in the
landscape of my life — "a sea change." And I want
everyone to know how positive that has been.*

— Maxine

It was mid-February and we both were very excited about the
upcoming trip because of Maxine's good results with her last
visit in March of 2002. This time I was going with her from the
start and she was very happy that I would be there for her. We
had made arrangements for me to be there for two weeks; then
a woman from our church was going to come down and stay
with her for a week; then Maxine's sister or daughter would
come down for a week or two. It was all planned out so that she
could stay as long as needed to regain some strength.

I made reservations at OHI for the first three weeks and
paid in advance to be sure we would not lose our room. Since

Maxine was having a hard time getting around and could not sit very comfortably, I purchased first class tickets for us and later I was sure glad I did.

It was so obvious that Maxine was getting weaker by the day, but I refused to see it; I looked the other way. I believe now that she knew she did not have much time left in this world and was putting on an act because she knew how I would be affected if she came out and told me. I did not want to see the truth, so I didn't. As I look back I am now able to see that during the last few months she did everything she could to protect me from what she knew was happening.

BACK TO SAN DIEGO

We had a very nice flight down to San Diego and this time I rented a car so that we could drive ourselves to Lemon Grove. Once there, we checked in and Maxine went to our room to rest awhile. The weather was beautiful and sure enough the hummingbirds were everywhere. After dinner that night she was feeling a little stronger, so we took a ride around town to do some sightseeing. The first time we had been there we had not seen much of the area outside the OHI grounds.

That first week went by fast and did seem to produce some good results. Maxine was able to do the morning exercises and eat her meals and even get around without the wheelchair at times. Not very far, but at least she was walking and seemed to be getting stronger. I admit my hopes were sky high by the end of that first week. I could see better color in her face and she was moving around more than before we came. The diet they serve there does wonders for a person. I was starting to believe that she may be able to go to Germany after all. The chemo had compromised her immune system, but she was recovering from it, or at least that's the way it seemed at the time.

The second week started off on a bad note as she began having more trouble breathing. She had been using an oxygen tank every so often at home to help with her breathing, but we had not been able to bring a portable machine with us. I had to take her to a doctor and get a prescription to have an oxygen machine brought into our room for her to use. That seemed to help give her more strength and allowed her to sleep better. Things began to decline rapidly by Wednesday of that week. She had a problem with her catheter and had to go to the hospital emergency room to get it changed. With that taken care of, she was feeling better and we returned to OHI.

Maxine wanted to go visit one of her oldest friends, who lived near Lemon Grove, so we drove around until I found her house. I was more than happy to sit in the car and allow them some time together with no one around. It made Maxine so happy and she had not been happy much in the prior three to six months. It didn't take long for her to be worn out. This is the point where I really started to see how bad she was getting.

OVERWHELMED

Later, back at OHI once she was asleep, I went outside and took a walk around the grounds. It was about 10:30 in the evening and I didn't want anyone to see me in tears, so I wandered around in the parking lot and out by the garden.

As I walked I was overwhelmed with a fear of losing her that was unreal. Again I had thoughts of running away and never looking back. I had to get a grip. Maxine would have no one to care for her if I left. Even if she did, I could never leave her when she trusted me so completely. Besides, as sick as she was, she was still the most beautiful woman in the world to me. The love I saw in her eyes each time I did something for her was enough to keep me there through whatever we would have to face. This woman really loved me with all her heart. We had truly become one when we were married, just as the Bible says we do. Most of the time I knew what she was thinking, just as she knew what I was thinking or even what I was going to say. We were that close. I took some deep breaths. I didn't really want to leave; my heart was simply being devastated by the condition my girl was in.

I would give any man this bit of advice: If you leave your wife in her time of need, you will be the loser in the end. What you will lose is the chance to see what I saw those last few months in the eyes of my bride. There was fear in her eyes of course, but there was more love than I had ever thought possible aimed directly at me and it was the greatest feeling I have ever experienced. If you leave her, you lose.

MORE COMPLICATIONS

The very next day we had another problem with the catheter and had to go back to the hospital. At that point Maxine's pain medicine was no longer doing the job and she needed something stronger. The doctor we were seeing at Grossmont Hospital was one of the nicest I have ever met. He was not about to let Maxine leave the hospital until he was sure that she was completely comfortable with the new catheter and pain medication. Before he released her he gave me his personal cell phone number and told me to call him if anything was needed. This was great because over the next three days I had to call him several times for advice and prescriptions. He never got upset and handled everything Maxine needed immediately. He was truly one of those you pray you will find.

IMPROVEMENT?

By Friday of the second week things had settled down a bit and Maxine was doing better. The medications were working well; the catheter was not creating a problem anymore. She was able to walk around the room and even go to some classes with me. She was going to exercise classes in her wheelchair and looked like a woman who was getting stronger. I had called home to let everyone know I was staying another week and the woman from our church did not need to come down. Maxine's sister was to be there at the end of the third week, and it appeared that things were getting better. She was eating each meal and talking and moving about better than she had since we had arrived. Again I began to hope she would regain strength and fight off the cancer. I guess I was living in a fool's paradise.

DINNER OUT

On Sunday, March 2nd, we had a very nice day and Maxine wanted to go out for dinner that night. I was surprised at this and asked her if she really wanted to eat something other than OHI food. She insisted we go out, so off we went to a local pizza joint. I was really surprised that she wanted pizza, but that was okay by me since I was tired of the raw food. We went inside and ordered and she was talking and smiling as if nothing was wrong at all. They brought us our pizza and I stuffed myself while she ate only one or two pieces. Even at that I thought she was doing well to eat so much after only having raw food for two weeks. Little did I know that this would be the last time we were out together for dinner or anything else.

I believe she somehow knew and that's why she had insisted on us going out. We were the only ones sitting in that restaurant. She was in a wheelchair with a beautiful scarf around her head to conceal that she had no hair, but still had that smile that lit up the room. I gazed at her and felt so much love that I could have burst. As sick and weak as she was she had not complained even once in weeks, and I knew she'd been in pain the entire time. It was so frustrating to be unable to take that pain away.

When we got back to the room she was very tired so I helped her get ready for bed. She was asleep in only a few minutes. I was awake for a long time looking at her and reading and wondering what was going to happen over the next few weeks.

A LIGHT SWITCH

The next morning I woke up and got cleaned up and ready to go and then went to wake up Maxine. She seemed unable to wake up completely. I knew that this was bad. I helped her dress and brush her teeth. I had to help her do everything. She was not even able to talk clearly to me. She was unable to do even the simplest exercise that day and I knew that the cancer had taken over completely.

Tuesday morning I called Aolani in Washington and told her to get down there as quickly as possible. It was as if someone had turned off a light switch. Maxine had gone from talking and even walking some the night before to completely helpless and immovable overnight.

Aolani arrived in San Diego Tuesday afternoon and I was so glad to see her since I was exhausted. I had been doing everything for Maxine since Monday morning. I arranged for the three of us to fly home Wednesday morning.

Aolani took care of Maxine while I got everything ready to go the next day. I had to ship a lot of things home and pack the car and check out and try to get the money back on the two next weeks, for which I had already paid. OHI was very understanding about it and refunded the money. They are wonderful people down there and helped us out as much as they could. All the while Maxine was barely able to speak.

Tuesday night the woman in charge of OHI nutrition, who is also a registered nurse, came to our room to see Maxine. She and Maxine had known each other since the first time Maxine was down there and they had become friends. She helped feed her that night, then took me outside and said, "I believe that Maxine is passing away."

I looked at her and barely was able to squeak out, "I know." I did know and I was dying inside. I knew that the end was very near but I denied it in my mind and in my heart. I didn't want to believe it and refused to give up hope. The reality of the situation was something I didn't want to face — I couldn't face.

CHAPTER 19

Coming Home the Last Time

◆ ◆ ◆

It has been good walking with Him. In spite of my
mistakes, failings, struggles and unwillingness —
He has taught me much. So much I long to share!
So much I want to live for! And yet I look forward
to Heaven in my heart more and more.

— Maxine

We left OHI for the airport early the next morning. Maxine was so weak by now that I had to pick her up to move her from the car to the wheelchair and back. Whenever I did she groaned, because no matter how I moved her it hurt her. It was tearing me up.

SECURITY

We checked in our baggage and then, of all things, we got tagged to go through some additional security screening. Agents frisked each of us. In doing so with Maxine, they hurt her.

"Hey!" I snarled. "What do you think you're doing?"

"We're required to do this, sir. I'm going to have to ask you to calm down."

I did, but not for long. We finally got to the terminal and as we were getting ready to board the plane, two agents pulled us off again for another complete search. This time I came unglued.

"What the hell is this? You're going to search her again?"

"Yes, sir" said the male agent. "We have to search you all again."

"You don't *have* to search my wife. She's already been searched."

"I'm sorry sir," said the female agent.

"So help me God if you hurt her I will hurt you and nothing you do can stop me."

The gate agent scurried over. "Sir, if you do not get yourself under control we will have to call security."

"I don't care who the hell you call. My wife is hurting enough and if you touch her I'll show you what pain is."

Aolani, much wiser than I, walked up and put her arm around me. "It's okay, Alan. I'm not going to let anyone hurt my mother and you can't do her any good in jail."

I took a breath and let it out. She was right.

The agent preparing to frisk Maxine looked over at me, then to the female agent and asked, "Um, do you want to search her?"

The female agent shook her head.

The male stood up and said, "Well, I'm not going to do it."

This was a good thing because I would have seriously injured someone had I thought they'd hurt Maxine again.

When I looked around I saw a number of passengers who had gotten up and started walking towards Maxine. I believe that if the agents had continued with their search, it wouldn't have been just me getting upset. Once they chose not to frisk her, everyone sat back down.

FLIGHT

When we got on the plane I had to pick Maxine up and place her in her seat and that caused her to groan in pain again. I felt so bad each time I had to do that because I could find no way to move her without hurting her and the pain pills were no longer keeping the pain down. Maxine needed extra room, so I had purchased first class tickets again. The attendants allowed Maxine and Aolani to sit in the first two seats since those seats had the most room to get Maxine in and out. I sat directly behind them. Thankfully the flight was very smooth and the attendants on Alaska Airlines were wonderful to us.

I had called ahead for Terry Newby to meet us at Sea-Tac Airport. Aolani's truck was in the parking lot and she was going to take everything home while Terry took Maxine and I straight to Swedish Medical Center where her doctor and had everything set up for her to be admitted. I had moved her from the wheelchair to the plane and then to the wheelchair and in and out of cars, and hurt her so many times I had to leave the room when it came time to put her in the bed. I was no longer able to see her in that much pain.

Keeping Vigil

Once settled and out of pain, she seemed to be comfortable and was even able to talk to us a little. Aolani and I had agreed to take turns staying overnight with her so that one of us was there all the time. Aolani was to be staying that first night so I could go home, unpack and get some sleep. Sometime during all of this, Aolani had called Maxine's sister, Eleana, in Dallas and she and Maxine's mother were coming up that weekend. It was now Wednesday, March 5, 2003.

The first couple nights that it was my turn to stay with Maxine, she would look at me and say, "I want to go to our home." It was so hard for me to tell her I was unable to allow that. I told her that I didn't have the equipment at home to take care of her. I finally made a deal with her that she accepted: I said that when she was strong enough to get up, put her clothes on and walk to the hospital door, I would take her home. She agreed to this (or at least she said she did) and never asked me again.

That night she kept talking in her sleep and waking me up. All she had to do was make a sound and I would be up and at her side in a second. It was plain to see that she was sound asleep but, as she had done the entire time we were married, she was talking just as clearly as if she were awake. I had no idea what she was talking about but she went on almost all night that one night.

Aolani and I continued to alternate nights spent with Maxine until Eleana arrived. Then it was only every third night, now that we had another person in the rotation. I don't believe any of us got much sleep during that time, even when we were at home. I know I didn't. I was feeling guilty whenever I went home to shave and clean up. I felt like I should have been there every second of the day and night. Although I know that it was unreasonable for me to feel this way I still did and it was a reality I had to deal with. My only way to make myself feel better was to get back to the hospital as soon as I possibly could.

For the first four or five days Maxine was able to talk every once in a while, but not very well. Her IV pain medication had to be kept so high it made her sleep most of the time. All we could do was be there and talk to her. I believe she was able to hear us because once in a while she would respond with a hand movement or a low "yes" when we asked her something. We tried to ask questions that could be answered with a yes or no. Occasionally Maxine would say a few words that we could understand, but those moments were brief.

During this time one of the most heart breaking things I have ever seen happened. My oldest son (Scott) had taken Maxine's little red Toyota pickup that she was so proud of over to his shop in Kennewick the day we left for OHI that last time. We wanted to surprise her so he was going to rebuild her truck and paint it for her. He had made that truck look brand new and even had a special bed liner sprayed in it. He and Tanya, his wife, came to the hospital with pictures of the truck, since I had told him Maxine would be unable to go down and look at it. I will never forget my 27-year-old son trying to show pictures of that truck to Maxine with tears running down his face. She was unable to see the pictures. He had wanted to do that for her for a couple years and was devastated that she could not enjoy it. I walked out with him and told him not to worry; that she knew very well what he had done for her and that she loved him for it.

Those next three or four days went by so fast that I can hardly remember them. I do remember her sister bringing in a small terrycloth snowman she had bought for Maxine. You see, Maxine loved snowmen, and had them all over the house at Christmas. I'm not sure if she was even able to see it at that time, but she knew what it was and grabbed onto it and never let go until she passed away.

My other two sons called a lot, asking how she was doing, and Bryan asked if he should come over to see her. I told him that because of the very special bond he and Maxine had, I didn't think he would want to remember her as she looked now, but that it would be up to him. He agreed and decided to stay in Ellensburg and take care of his schoolwork and job.

Chris (23) also felt he wanted to remember Maxine as she was, but then changed his mind and came for a short visit one evening. I wasn't there when Aolani took Chris up to see Maxine, but I understand it was emotional.

My sister Wilma and her husband Larry came over to see Maxine and stayed one night at our house. I was thankful for them coming because Maxine knew that they were there even if her eyes were not open, and she had always been happy to see them. All day, every day and evening there was a steady stream of people coming into her hospital room to see her. Many I had never seen before, but I was so glad to have them come. Maxine knew when they were there and responded as she could with a small hand signal or faint "yes" or "no."

Each time I went home I wanted to smash things; I wanted to scream. I wanted help and I didn't know what kind of help I wanted or needed, maybe just someone to hang onto. I had never felt so lost and helpless in my life.

LETTING GO

Tuesday evening, March 11th, it was my turn to stay with Maxine. About 10:30 that evening everyone had left and I was going to try to get some sleep when I heard Maxine groaning in pain. I got up from the little bed that was there for us and looked at her face. Even with the strong IV pain medication I could see that she was hurting. At that moment something came over me that I cannot explain. I had to do something that would let her go. I wasn't sure what it was, so I stood there looking at her and praying for some kind of guidance.

Whether it was something I thought of or it was put into my mind from God, I'm not sure, but I suddenly knew what I had to do. I leaned over and kissed her on the cheek and whispered into her ear. I said, *"Maxine, you are the love of my life and always will be, but I can no longer stand to see you in such pain, baby. I want you to know that I release you to go to Jesus and be with Him, as you always wanted to be. I wanted you with me forever, but I release you from any vow you still hold onto. I love you, baby; you will always be my girl, my blonde. I love you."*

Let me tell you, that was the hardest thing I had ever done in my life. Maxine was worried about me more than herself, and had even asked her sister to take care of Aolani and me. She was hanging onto her life and her pain for us when she needed to be free of that pain.

TIME TO GO

I lay down then and was able to sleep, for she never made another sound until morning. About 7:00 AM I woke up and washed and went over to her bed and she seemed to be sleeping peacefully. I was about to walk away to get a cup of coffee when she said to me, "Time to go."

I was not sure just what that meant at the time but she said it several times over the next couple hours. A few days earlier she had sat up and grabbed both Aolani's and her sister's hands and told them that she was scared. Now she was telling me that it was time to go with a very peaceful look on her face. I believe that there were more in that room than Maxine and I. I was unable to see who it was, but she could.

Aolani and Maxine's sister arrived to take over at about 10:00 AM and I had to go home and get cleaned up to meet my brother who was driving over from Richland to see Maxine. Since it was Wednesday, I told him that I wanted to take him to a Point Man meeting that night also.

It was about 5:30 that night when my brother and I got to the hospital again. Maxine was breathing very heavily and something did not look right to me. I held her hand and tried looking into her eyes and I knew she was gone. Her body was still breathing and working but I knew she was no longer there. I very carefully removed her wedding ring and placed it in my pocket. Then I looked at my brother and said, "Let's go to Point Man." I needed to see those guys and be with them, and I needed it right then. They would be the only ones that I knew of who would understand how I felt.

We left the hospital and I was numb. I knew I had lost my best friend. I had to get to that meeting because I know she would have wanted me to be there.

The meeting was normal for most of the guys, but it was far from that for me; it was my hiding place and they were my relief. I attempted to hide how I felt and how much pain I was in at the time. I think some of them sensed the pain and they all prayed for me and for Maxine. The guys heard a little about my brother who had been in Nam and was 100% disabled from that war and had to walk with a cane. They really enjoyed a couple stories he had to tell and prayed for him also. It was a great night with the best men in the world. These are the true American heroes that you never see or hear of on TV or in the newspaper.

When the meeting was over it was about 9:00 PM. We went back up to the hospital and found that nothing had changed. Maxine was still breathing very heavily, or at least her body was.

It was Aolani's night to stay so my brother and I left to go to my place to get some sleep. I was to be back up there in the morning, but I already knew that I would not be needed. We had gotten to my place and had just gone to sleep when the phone rang. I knew before I even answered it who it was and why. It was Aolani. "Mom's gone," she said.

Leave-taking

I told her I would be right up there. It was about 12:15 AM, March 13, 2003. Maxine had stopped breathing just a few minutes after midnight. Even having known earlier in the day, the actual words still cut through me and I was like a zombie driving back up there.

Everything I had dreaded and feared for three and a half years had happened. I could no longer deny it to myself and tell myself that it would never happen. My thoughts went back to the day I first met this beautiful woman and I was able to recall almost every day of our life together. I remembered that first year and a half before the cancer when we had about everything a couple could want and were looking forward to a wonderful future. I recalled finding the lump and how we had fought so hard to find a way for her to be healed.

I remembered my original thoughts of *how am I going to*

make it without this woman when we first found the lump. I remembered some of the silly things, like how proud I was of her when she was on stage at her 30-year class reunion and got a kiss on the cheek from J.P. Patches. All of this and more was going through my mind as I drove back to that hospital.

I don't think my brother and I said anything the entire thirty-minute drive. Once there, we went up the elevator and I headed toward her room even though I didn't want to. I was unable to stop. I walked into the room and saw her body lying there not breathing and I lost everything. The nurses had put warm blankets on Maxine's hands to keep them warm for me to hold and say good-bye one last time.

I picked up her small, lifeless body and pulled her to me as tight as I could and I cried. It seemed like I could not stop. The three and a half years of pain came out all at once and I was more lost than I had ever been. Aolani came over to me and put her arm around my shoulder.

I don't even know how long I was there crying before I was able to let go and look up. When I did, it was just Aolani and me in the room. By this time Aolani had walked to the other side of the bed and kneeled down beside her mother. As I looked at this beautiful young woman I could see Maxine in her so well. It hit me right then that she was also hurting and probably even more than I.

"Aolani, I am so sorry." I walked over to her, put my arm around her and pulled her to me.

She began to cry and I just stood there holding her because

it was the first time since the very beginning I had seen this young woman cry. She was as strong as her mother and now she would have to go on without her. It didn't seem right to me for her to have to do that.

Aolani and I stayed in the room for a while with Maxine before we were able to cover her up and start picking up her things. I believe we were both working on reflex and didn't really know what we were doing. Maxine's sister and my brother came back in and everyone retrieved all of their things. I talked to the nurse about where Maxine's body was going and what I would need to do in the morning. I would have to call back the next morning since I could not remember anything that they had told me anyway.

My brother and I left and headed to my place, but stopped to get some breakfast before going home. Once I got home I tried to sleep, but it was not happening. I was only beginning to realize that I would never see her again and that she would never be coming home. Even today, I find myself having a hard time believing this. I guess it's more like not wanting to believe it.

THINGS TO REMEMBER:

◆ I believe that if you are ever in that situation, you must be able to let your loved one know that it is all right for her to go. You must release her and you must tell her that you do. But you must do it in love and make sure she knows that too. It could be that you are the only reason she is hanging on and staying in pain.

CHAPTER 20

The Memorial

◆ ◆ ◆

Blessed are they that mourn, for they shall be comforted.
— Matthew 5:4

A memorial was decided on the day after Maxine died. It would be held on March 17 at a borrowed church out in Maple Valley. Our church always met in the gym of a school, so we had to ask another church if we could use theirs for the service. Again, New Community Church came to our rescue. They organized everything and, working with Aolani and Maxine's sister, put together a great memorial. I was in shock and was not much use to anyone the three days prior to the 17th, so I left town to go visit my son Scott, his wife Tanya and my grandkids.

GOING THROUGH THE MOTIONS

While in Kennewick, Scott and I cleaned up and painted a new canopy that I had purchased for Maxine's truck. It was another gift that she never got to see. Before I left I had placed all of Maxine's and my pictures out on the front room floor of my house for Aolani and Maxine's sister to go through for the slide show. I also gave Aolani enough money for the memorial since I did not want anyone else having to pay for anything. I know I left them completely stuck with all the work, but I was not up to it and needed to leave for a couple days.

The two days and nights Scott and I worked on that canopy were very helpful in allowing me to work through my private thoughts that kept going back to Maxine and how much I already missed her. I had not really accepted the fact that she was gone yet. I expected to hear my cell phone ring and hear her asking when I would be home with her truck.

Scott wanted me to stay at his home while I was there. He was a little disappointed that I insisted on getting a hotel room. I found that I wanted to be alone at night and did not even understand why. During the day it was okay having people around, but at night I did not want anyone near me.

We got the canopy painted Saturday night and on the truck by Sunday afternoon, so I was able to head home about five in the afternoon.

SAVE THE LAST DANCE

On Sunday during my drive home I suddenly had an idea. I called Aolani and asked her if she would come up on stage and dance with me during the slide show of Maxine's life. The slide show was being shown to the song, "My Heart Will Go On" from the movie *Titanic*. Maxine and I had danced to this song at our wedding reception.

When I told her what I wanted to do, she told me she'd have to think about it. I told her I wanted to keep this between us and only tell people on a "need-to-know basis."

When I got home Sunday night Aolani called me to say that she would do it, but that she had never danced in the manner for which this song called. My son Chris had been taking ballroom dance classes for a year or two. He met us at the church for a dance lesson. Within an hour, you would never have guessed that Aolani had not danced before. She caught on fast, and after we went through the entire song twice with no problems, I told her she was ready. She was worried about dancing in front of a crowd of people, but Chris and I told her that the people would be watching the slide show, not us, and that seemed to help.

GENTLE LAUGHTER

Everything was in place for Maxine's memorial service on Monday, March 17th, and all I had to do was rehearse what I was going to say so well that I could do it in my sleep.

I had made a list of about 10 things that had happened to us over the years that were humorous and I knew people would enjoy hearing —things like the time Maxine found my stash of Oreo cookies and threw them on the floor and jumped up and down on them in her bathrobe! I had this on video and it was hard for even my friend Terry to believe she would do that until he saw it. I also recalled the time she hid all the chocolate chip cookies in a container in the freezer labeled "tofu pups." I had looked for those cookies for a month without being able to find them. She would only give me two a day, and I could not figure out where she had hidden them. You see, I have a real weakness for homemade chocolate chip cookies.

The reason for my nervousness was that I was still not able to even talk about Maxine without choking up completely. I wanted the memorial to be light-hearted and not just a somber event.

REMEMBERING

The place was nearly full. Hundreds of her friends from all over came to remember Maxine. Pastor Ken opened the memorial and spoke for a bit and then the music pastor, Shaun, and his band played several of the songs he had written. Maxine loved Shaun's music and songs and I wanted only the ones she loved played that day. The songs he chose were perfect.

Once they were done, Pastor Ken introduced the people who were going to come to up and speak. Aolani was first and she talked about how perfect life was when she was very small — how at night she could hear her mom on the sewing machine and know the next morning she would have some brand new creation to wear. Maxine could sew and create just about anything.

Her brother got up and spoke about how Maxine was now in Heaven and in the fullness of joy and that she would never want to come back. I had to agree with him, for she certainly deserved that joy.

The next speaker surprised me because I had no idea what he was about to do. My dear friend Terry, to everyone's surprise, talked about me. He said I had been an inspiration to the men in Point Man by showing them how a man stays completely loyal to his wife. He had the guys from Point Man stand up — about 10 or 12 of them were there. I was so taken aback by this that I was not sure if I would be able to go up and speak. I did manage to get up there and do my thing, and even got the crowd to laugh through most of it. That was fitting because Maxine would have liked to see people having a good time rather than being sad.

After I was done talking, Ken came up and spoke for a while again. Thank God for Ken because he really kept the memorial going smoothly. He led us in a wonderful prayer and turned it over to me again. I had been able to compose myself by then and got up to announce the slide show.

"'My Heart Will Go On' is the song Maxine and I started our life together with at our wedding. Today I want to ask her lovely daughter, my stepdaughter, to join me on the stage to take her mother's place — just for a few moments — to finish our life with the same dance."

I don't think too many people expected that to happen and

as she walked up it appeared to me that it had affected most everyone in the room. Aolani and I had planned the dance to end just seconds before the last slide was shown. (That slide was a picture of Maxine and me kissing that Maxine had cut into a heart shape.) The idea was that we would stop and stand there looking at that last slide together.

It worked perfectly, and as I hugged her I told her, "I love you as much as any of my sons."

"I love you, too," she said.

I never had a daughter and I now knew that it was something I had missed out on. I couldn't have asked for a better stepdaughter. Her mother may be gone, but Aolani will always be one of my kids. My sons all consider her to be their sister and I don't believe that will ever change.

THE LIVES SHE TOUCHED

Thanks to New Community Church, Pastors Ken and Shaun, and our families, the memorial was an incredible success. Many people stayed long after, talking and having refreshments. I was able to meet many people for the first time who had touched Maxine's life. It was fun finding out how she had never changed. From the time she was young she was always as cheerful and full of fun as she was in the short time she was in my life.

Several came up to me and told me that she had led them to the Lord, the same as she did me. I even got to talk to the gentleman who, many years ago as a teenager, had led Maxine to the Lord. He had been at the Germany fundraiser a few months earlier, but I did not get a chance to talk to him at that time. He was a very sweet man and had a great family. I wish I had been able to get to know them better.

There were many people at the memorial who had known Maxine but who I did not know. I was unable to get around to meeting all of them. I was sorry I couldn't talk to every person there since I was hearing great stories about her from each one I did manage to meet. I could have listened to them for hours.

Once everything was over, the church staff and volunteers told me that they would clean everything up. They wouldn't let me help at all and I guess that was a good idea. I wasn't feeling the best and I'm sure they didn't need anything broken because I wasn't paying attention. So I left and had dinner with my closest friends, Terry, Susan, Doug and Janet. All my kids had taken off to go eat with others and that was okay.

ALONE

After dinner I drove to our little rental house and looked around the front room at all the pictures of Maxine. I don't know how long I stood there before falling down on the floor, but that is where I stayed for a couple hours holding one of her pictures and crying, wishing with all my heart that she was there with me. I was lost and had no idea how I was going to make it without her. I had put up a good front (or so I thought) for five days now and I needed to let it out. I lay there with that picture realizing a new life had to start now, for I had no choice.

THINGS TO REMEMBER:

◆ You may find yourself wanting to be alone at night and not understanding why. I believe that there is nothing wrong with this and that it is a natural feeling. Everyone is different, so do what feels right to you.

CHAPTER 21

Three Years after Loss

◆ ◆ ◆

Consider it pure joy, my brothers, whenever you face
trials of many kinds, because you know that the testing
of your faith develops perseverance. Perseverance must
finish its work so that you may be mature and complete,
not lacking anything. If any of you lacks wisdom, he
should ask God, who gives generously to all without
finding fault, and it will be given to him.
— James 1:2-5

It has been three years since I lost Maxine to breast cancer and the story keeps going. Many times I think about what I could say to another man who is in the position I was in

THE WILDERNESS OF GRIEF

Everyone I knew told me to take some time off from work and try to get over it. That didn't work for me and I suspect it won't work for a lot of the men who read this book. I truly wish

I could tell you that time cures the problem, but it really doesn't. After six months I was still missing her as much as ever. The joy, the fun, the excitement were gone. I was at home all alone and wondering what the future would hold for me.

For the first couple of months I just worked, came home and went to the gym to lift weights or do cardio. I had to keep doing something because whenever I had idle time I would almost lose control of myself. I would become nearly hysterical with grief and be hitting and kicking things. I kept waking up in the night, expecting to have her next to me, then realizing she would never be there again.

Oh did I ever put on a good front for everyone at work and all of my friends. Yes, I could make anyone believe that I was handling it very well. I was almost finished with my Masters degree in Business and I only had two more classes to get my Masters in Public Administration when Maxine died. She had wanted to see me graduate more than anyone. Now, I was continuing with the last of my classes because I know she would have wanted me to, but I had no drive or motivation at all. I was doing it because it was habit. Even when I finished, that joy that I had always waited for simply was not there. I was unable to even bring myself to go to my graduation.

I'm still not sure how I'm supposed to feel now, but I can tell you that often it still feels like it just happened. I drive out to the cemetery where her ashes are and when I see her name up on that wall I cannot even stand up. I sit down on the concrete and stare up at her name wishing that it wasn't there. I guess I will never really "get over" her now that she's gone. I miss everything about her.

I have many pictures of her up on my "memory wall." I have been able to take down the picture of her that I had taped to the dash of my truck, but sometimes I even miss that. When I open my wallet to pay for something people often ask me about the picture I keep there. I find myself talking about her almost every day. I still break down and cry sometimes when I look at her picture.

If I stop and sit for too long a time I begin to think about Maxine and it seems as if everything is happening all over again fresh. A song on the radio or even seeing a woman with long, blonde, wavy hair can set me off and I am a mess. Maxine is so vivid in my mind that all the pain from the loss comes flowing back like a tidal wave and I lose it. This happens at church many times when they sing one of her favorite songs. One song in particular makes me leave the room. It creates so many memories that the pain is overwhelming.

THE DANGER ZONE

You may experience loneliness after your loss and that can drive you to excessive behavior. No one knew that I was in a bar every night that first year sitting alone and drinking. I didn't talk to anyone and didn't want anyone talking to me. I was later told that a number of people in the bar were afraid of me because of the way I looked and acted.

I believe it was the loneliness that drove me to the bar. Even though I did not want anyone to talk to me, I would sit there and listen to the music and watch people. I simply did not want to be in the house alone. In a way this may have been good for me. At least I was not hiding out at home alone and drinking myself into oblivion. I always knew I had to drive home so I never drank enough to get drunk, although some nights I really wanted to.

I would not propose to tell a grieving man not to go out and have a drink; however, from what I have learned, I would suggest he find someone who has been through it and ask him to go along. Having someone to talk to who knows the pain may keep the drinks down and make the loneliness a little easier to bear.

Now and again I would get an urge to do something like ride my son's motorcycle at high speed (135 plus) down a highway. At the time I knew what I was doing was stupid, but I still did it. I probably should not even tell about it, but If I don't I'm not being honest with you. I know you will feel like doing something like that and I want you to know you are not alone. My advice is to call someone like myself and talk about it instead; that's what I do anymore.

"Trigger" Times

I find myself having a hard time around anniversary dates such as the date she died, her birthday and our wedding date. I have trouble sleeping and I get grouchy.

Two months after her death was May 24th — both our wedding anniversary and her birthday. As we approached that day, I was getting less sleep and having a very tough time keeping my mind on anything other than Maxine. My sons knew this date was coming and all three of them showed up at my house the day before. They informed me that they would be staying around all day on the 24th. Aolani called on the phone to check in. They had all figured it was going to be a hard day for me, so they made sure that I had plenty to do with them. It was great and we had a good time even though it was a sad day for all of us. I was very glad that they took the time out of their busy schedules to be with me.

CABO

I had one very bright spot in that first six months in June, 2003. I was able to keep a promise to my two youngest sons: a reward for them giving so generously of their hard-earned money for Maxine's treatments, even when it could have cost them a full year of school. The week that classes finished for the summer I told them to pack a bag for a full week in Cabo San Lucas, Mexico. They had never really had a vacation, and even when we got to Cabo, Bryan said that he could hardly believe it. Chris and Bryan were 24 and 21, respectively, and had never even been on a commercial airliner up to that point.

I had reserved a suite with a hot tub on the balcony through my Trend West membership. I rented a car and gave each of the guys a thousand dollars. I told them that I was just the driver that week and I could not see, hear or say anything. That week was for them to do as they wanted and have fun. Wow! What a wild place that was. I had never seen anything like the clubs in Cabo. Every night but one the guys kept me out until 3:00 or 4:00 AM before wanting to go back to the room.

On the last morning of our trip we were having breakfast and chatting about the great time we'd had. We were discussing a 200-plus pound Blue Fin Marlin that Chris had caught and released a couple days earlier. Just as breakfast was placed on the table, the overhead music started playing very softly, "My Heart Will Go On."

I started to ask the guys if they knew what was playing. Before the words left my mouth, I realized Chris and Bryan were unusually focused on eating, both trying to hide the tears running down their cheeks.

After the song, I asked them a question I'd been wondering about all week, "Guys, I agreed to drive and not see, hear or tell about anything that took place in Cabo. You've both had a thousand chances to not come home with me at night. Why have the two of you come to the room every night with me?"

They both looked up at me. "Well," said Bryan, "we promised Maxine we would."

Chris nodded.

I was surprised, proud and devastated at the same time. That woman had such an impact on my family in the short time she was with us. I had always taught my sons that if a man did not keep his word, he was nothing. Now here were my two sons keeping their word to their stepmother even months after her death. What more could a father ever ask?

MAXINE'S HOPE

Maxine had always wanted my sons to become Christians. She was working on them the entire time she knew them, but had not succeeded by the time she left us. I wanted to carry on that effort, so I decided to buy each of them and my daughter-in-law a new Bible and have their name engraved on the cover in gold. I sent them each their Bible, along with a personal letter explaining what Maxine and I had wanted: to bring each of them to the Lord and baptize them at our church. I told them that it was too late for Maxine to be there, but I would ask Aolani to help me baptize them when the time came. I told them that all I asked was that they read the New Testament and make up their own minds as to what they believed. Once they have read it I will accept whatever decision they make. I know that at least two of the four are reading and I am waiting.

New Community Church was as responsible as anyone for my sons even considering Jesus. As my son Chris told me one day a few months after Maxine's death, "The church backed you on everything you and Maxine did. Your other friend's church donated money to you for OHI twice and didn't even know you. I never knew any church would do such things. On top of all that your Christian friends were always there for you. Maybe I need to look into this Christian stuff a little closer."

I was so shocked by his statement because of all my sons I always thought Chris would be the toughest to convince. And as always, it comes down to not what we say, but how we act, what we do, and who we are. The daily actions of true Christians probably bring more converts than all the words that have ever been spoken on the subject. The actions of New Community and the Koppangs' church had gotten to my son's heart where no amount of words from Maxine or myself had.

HOW ARE WE NOW?

Bryan is going to school in Georgia at the Savannah School of Art and Design. He is an incredible artist (his work is on the cover of this book) and wants to be an animator. He was thrilled to have sold his first oil painting this last year to a gentleman from Bellevue, Washington for $750. The man told us he wanted the painting because he knew what it would be worth in the future.

Recently an art dealer told Bryan not to sell any more originals. He photographed Bryan's remaining original paintings so that he could sell prints on the Net. As good as his oil paintings are, in my opinion they don't compare to the work he does with cartoons.

Bryan is my only son remaining single at this time. I believe he still compares every girl he meets to Maxine and/or his step-sister, who is so much like her mother. He has told me many times that he would like to meet a girl with the same values and appeal that Maxine had. Well, I sure can't fault him for that.

Chris, my middle son is 27 now and married to a great girl who is a Christian. Wow! What a change in a young man. When he first met Maxine he didn't even want to continue living. He was mad at the world and hated almost everything. Now, he is cheerful and fun to be around. He has just graduated from college with honors and a degree in finance and economics. He has several companies making offers to him and I couldn't be more proud.

My oldest son Scott is still living in Kennewick, Washington with his wife Tanya and their three children. We talk on the phone every second or third day. Each year he is my for-sure hunting partner since the other sons have been busy with school. Scott and I usually spend about a week up in the woods sleeping in a tent or sometimes a trailer and having a great time. Once in a while we even get a deer or an elk.

Aolani, my stepdaughter, lives in Fernley, Nevada with her husband, Josh. They have two dogs, plus "Muffin," the pukey cat who refuses to die. Josh is in the Navy; she is a mortgage broker for Wachovia and seems to love her work. We keep in touch by phone and e-mail and see each other a few times each year. It's tough when they live a long way away. I drove down there to see her at the end of June this year and delivered a long overdue wedding gift: an antique love seat that Maxine cherished, which I'd had re-upholstered. Aolani is very good at organizing and she rode home with me to help Chris and Kim plan their wedding.

I keep in close touch with all of my kids; this is one thing I have found helps relieve some of the pain.

I'm working, but I have not been able to get myself moving and get my business going anymore. Maxine was my office manager and she even went out on projects once in a while and inspected them for me. We did very well and she kept everything running smoothly in the office. I did find myself in a bit of a fix one day a year ago when a local city asked me to do a couple hours of work for them and I ended up doing it for free.

They told me to bill them, but I could not figure out on the computer how Maxine would bill them. It's rather bad when you can't even bill for your work. So I have not been working under my business name for some time now and don't know if I ever will be able to again. Finding something else to do may have been a good thing for me because I'm not reminded of her as much. Maybe you should look into a change of what you have been doing. It may change your state of mind.

On the other hand, it's interesting that my favorite recreation is still the things Maxine and I used to do together. I like to fish and hunt and hike in the woods. Going to Ocean Shores and digging razor clams is a special treat for me and I make sure I get to go every time the Fish and Game Department opens the beaches.

I've always enjoyed these things, but I feel close to Maxine now while I'm doing them. Each activity holds special memories and allows me to relax more than any other time. So don't stop doing all the things you and your wife loved to do.

DATING

About three months after I lost Maxine, a woman that I had known for a couple years asked me if I'd like to go out for dinner with her. After she asked me several times, I agreed. We had a nice dinner and talked for a considerable time before leaving the restaurant and sitting in her car to talk more. After about 15 minutes of chatting she informed me that she was married. Now this set me back a bit, and I asked her if maybe that was something she should have told me before we went to dinner. She did not see it as a problem, but I sure did. I left went home and decided dating was out of the picture for a long time after that.

Months later I met a woman who was very nice and loved to work out just like myself. She was a dark-haired beauty and I enjoyed her company, but I couldn't feel anything inside anymore. You see, one night a few months before I lost Maxine, she had looked up at me and said, "I can't tolerate the idea of you with another woman."

This statement haunts me day and night. I hear it every time I so much as look at a woman, and I have been unable to get it out of my head. I know that Maxine said it in the last days because she was so hurt to leave me. I also know that she would want me to be happy, because that's the way she was. However, knowing that and getting the statement out of my mind are two different things.

After three months the woman informed me that she could no longer be around with me showing no emotion. As time passed I found myself missing her and wishing that I could have felt something.

For the last year I have been seeing a woman and just having fun. However, again I am in a position where I find myself void of feelings. I have not been able to get past that. She's very sweet and kind but I find myself at night alone thinking about Maxine and I still love her as much as the day I met her. I told this woman from the day I met her what my situation was — that I didn't know if I would ever be able to feel anything towards another woman. She said that she understood and has been very good about it, but I can tell she is getting frustrated with me. I refuse to lie to her and say something I don't feel, so I continue on and simply wait and see what will happen.

FORGIVENESS

Nearly a year after Maxine died, a buddy at Point Man took me aside. He saw that I was being eaten up by thoughts of revenge on several people. The things I was thinking about I would have done with no feeling at all. "This is destroying you," he said.

He gave me a book called *Total Forgiveness* by R.T. Kendall. Once I read it I finally understood what Maxine had been trying to get across to me all the years we were married.

In the Lord's Prayer, Jesus told us to pray, "Forgive us our debts, as we also have forgiven our debtors." He went on to say, "For if you forgive men when they sin against you, your heavenly Father will also forgive you. But if you do not forgive men their sins, your Father will not forgive your sins." (Matthew 6:12, 14-15) This tells me that *forgiveness is the single most important thing the Bible is trying to get across.*

Once I learned *how* to forgive, I started buying copies of R.T. Kendall's book. I hand it out to everyone I know.

REACHING OUT

I have several friends who refer men to me whose wives have cancer. I talk to them the way I would have liked. I don't speak down to them when they cry or get incoherent. I was there many times, but had no one who understood. Sure, I had my friends, family and church but it's not like having someone who has been through it.

I want these men to see and understand that even while we will be praying for the best, they can still survive the worst. God says that you are stronger than you think and that he will not put more on you than you can bear. I believe he really tested me to the outermost limit of what I could bear; I am still so very hurt by it. However, if I can use the pain to provide for other men and help them through, then I will be doing something I know Maxine would want me to do.

Once I started writing and thinking of how I could help other men, I was able to direct my grief in a more positive way. I got more involved in helping others rather than burrowing into my own problems.

A lot of men who have experienced this type of loss have simply gone about their lives with no outlet. Men are so good at stuffing their pain, but it always seems to come out in another manner.

Keep in mind that your pain and feelings are a natural reaction to an un-natural experience. I know some will say that cancer is a natural experience, but I can't place it on the natural shelf when I see a very healthy young woman cut down in the prime of her life. I can only call it un-natural.

Go over to the home of someone who knows — or to a group of guys in a closed room, where you can talk openly with no inhibitions and know that whatever is said will never leave the room. It may be just what you need. I, for one, know it will help you if you try it.

Conclusion: The Challenge

◆ ◆ ◆

Rejoice with them that do rejoice,

and weep with them that weep.

— Romans 12:15

In the preceding chapters you have read about what I went through during the last five years. There is no way to put into writing all the emotions I experienced and I would bet you are dealing with too. My goal now is to continue in the support of those who have cancer, or a loved one with cancer.

Support groups are now being established for husbands who need to talk to another man who knows first-hand what it's like to have a spouse with this devastating disease or one like it. I would like to see chapters or groups in every city in this country and around the world. Contact me if you are interested in participating. Men are greatly needed who are willing to facilitate groups. No expertise is needed – just an ability to listen and be real. If you are interested in forming a group, your responsibilities would be to a) find a place to meet, b) schedule and spread the word, c) raise money to continue, and d) make a time commitment. Please contact me with your meeting information so that I can support you and send others your way.

The second undertaking will be a foundation to help people with health problems, such as cancer, when they choose to use natural treatments. Very little natural health treatment is covered by insurance and I believe that a foundation could get financial backing from many sources, such as churches, personal donations, corporations, and maybe the medical community fringe. This would give people the ability to pay their bills and obtain treatment when they need it. Needing treatment for your wife and not being able to afford it is a very disheartening experience. I know because I was in that position for a long time. I believe this country's insurance and health programs are far too expensive and do not deliver the range of services that people need. When treatments are too expensive, patients are forced to choose between health and house payments, power, water, kids, etc. I believe a foundation could help relieve that burden.

I would love to hear from you. If the response is strong enough, we can do something to help a lot of hurting people who don't know what to do or where to turn for help. I would appreciate a letter to the following address:

Alan E. Lobdell

P.O. Box 7600, Covington, WA 98031

Or email me at Alvanos@juno.com

Bibliography

◆ ◆ ◆

MATERIAL YOU MAY WANT TO READ BEFORE TREATMENT

Moss, Ralph W. PhD., *Questioning Chemotherapy*, Equinox Press, 1995

Huggins, Hal A., DDS, MS and Thomas E. Levy, MD, JD, *Uninformed Consent*, Hampton Roads Publishing Company, Inc., 1999

Regehr Clark, Hulda, PhD, ND, *The Cure For All Cancers*, New Century Press, 1993

Anderson, Greg, *The Cancer Conqueror*, Andrews McMeel Publishing, 2000

Frahm, Anne E. with Frahm, David J., *A Cancer Battle Plan*, Tarcher/Putnam, 1997

Ziff, Sam, Ziff, Michael F., DDS, and Hanson, Mats, PhD, *Dental Mercury Detox*, Bio Probe, Inc., 1997

Pearce, Ian C.B., BA, BM, BCh, MRCS, LRCP, *The Holistic Approach To Cancer*, C. W. Daniel Company, 2004

Naiman, Ingrid, *Cancer Salves*, Seventh Ray Press, 1999

Bratman, Steven, MD, *The Alternative Medicine Sourcebook*, Keats Publishing, 1999

Jochems, Ruth, *Dr. Moerman's Anti-Cancer Diet*, Avery Publishing Group, 1990

Keuneke, Robin, *Total Breast Health*, Kensington Publishing Corporation, 1999

Crook, William G., MD, *The Yeast Connection Handbook*, Professional Books, 2002

Crook, William G., MD, and Marjorie Hurt Jones, RN, *The Yeast Connection Cookbook*, Professional Books, 2001

Walters, Richard, *Options, The Alternative Cancer Therapy Book*, Avery Publishing Group Inc., 1993

Austin, Steve, ND and Hitchcock, Cathy, MSW, *Breast Cancer, What You Should Know (But May Not Be Told) About Prevention, Diagnosis, and Treatment*, Prima Publishing, 1994

Simontacchi, Carol, *The Crazy Makers*, Tarcher, 2001

Gottlieb, Bill, Ed., *New Choices in Natural Healing*, Rodale Press, Inc., 1995

Yeager, Selene and the editors of Prevention Magazine, *"New Foods for Healing,"* Bantam Books, 1999

Malkmus, George H., Rev., and Dye, Michael, *God's Way to Ultimate Health*, Hallelujah Acres Publishing, 1995

Thomas, Richard, *The Essiac Report*, Immunocorp, 1994

Willard, Terry, PhD, *Helping Yourself with Natural Remedies*, CRCS Publications, 1986

Calbom, Cherie and Keane, Maureen, *Juicing For Life,*, Avery Publishing Group, Inc., 1992

Meyerowitz, Steve, *Wheat Grass, Nature's Finest Medicine*, Sproutman Publications, 1999

Miller, Neil Z., *Vaccines: Are They Really Safe and Effective?*, New Atlantean Press, 1992

Balch, Phyllis A., CNC and Balch, James F., MD, *Prescription for Nutritional Healing*, Avery Publishing, 2000

OTHER USEFUL BOOKS

Kendall, R.T., *Total Forgiveness,* Charisma House Publishing, 2002

Dean, Chuck, *Nam Vet*, ACW Press, 2000